# BULLETPROOF

Building Better Employee Benefits

# BULLETPROOF

## Building Better Employee Benefits

DANIELLE WARNER

**BULLETPROOF: Building Better Employee Benefits**

Book Editing and Production:  Front Rowe Seat, karen@karenrowe.com
Cover Design: Shake Creative, www.ShakeTampa.com

ISBN: 978-981-09-8674-2

Printed in Singapore

*To Simon*

For always shining a light toward true North
but allowing me to navigate my own way there.

# Table of Contents

## Acknowledgements

There is an ecosystem of people whom believe in me and in my vision.

Creating this timeline, starting at the beginning, helps me thank each and every one of you. From when I was just a girl with an idea to those who continue to help fuel my disruption of today:

Thank you.

Mom
You showed me what it means to really believe in something.

| | |
|---|---|
| Leonard & Naomi | Block |
| Cheryl | Esterly |
| Stephen | Blasina |
| Adeline | Liew |
| Philip | Pomford |
| My Team | True Blue, Old & New |
| Jacqueline | Madley |
| Russell | Paul |
| Mark | Aliprantis |
| Amanda | Edwards |
| Tze Shin | Choong |
| Theresa | Fitzpatrick |
| Edouard | Lesellier |
| Parvathi | Narayan |
| Doina | Palici-Chehab |
| Phil | Austin |
| Khue | Dinh |
| Martin | Garcia |
| The KPI Crew | Callum Laing |
| | Daniel Priestley |
| | KPIs all over the world |
| My muse since May 2015 | John Gordon |
| Rob | McIntyre |
| Jonathan | O'Byrne |
| Gina Romero | you helped me put the icing on top |

# Section 1

## BRAVE NEW WORLD

# Introduction

## SAILING TO SAFE HARBOUR

The balance of power in the employment landscape has changed forever.

We are living in an era where employees are taking to the driver's seat, while the majority of employers remain frozen in time. Turnover is growing globally, at an alarming and costly rate. Employees are your newest customer - and they are demanding more than ever. Talent attraction has become a courtship and we have entered a new age where employees view their relationship with their employer as a partnership. To gain an edge, employers need to respond differently or risk entering a tailspin of trouble. You need to create an employee value proposition that can not only empower your brand, but also offer a powerful promise to the people that are helping to grow your business.

Whether you are a team of eight or eight thousand, keeping employee benefit programmes aligned with your organization, your people, your leadership, your goals and your competition, requires you to stay committed to a blueprint when building an effective benefits structure. Defining your HR and Benefits Philosophy, developing a customized benefits table, creating an infrastructure, empowering employees and reviewing the programme annually helps you deliver a sustainable and successful solution.

In my line of work, I hear horror stories on a daily basis. From a harrowing tale of a company whose health insurance coverage was not yet in place when an employee reported a dog bit his face, to the shock and awe of big ticket bills that followed an uncovered cancer claim, I've heard stories that will make your head spin. Insurance has become an industry that is legendary for being complex, tedious, and sometimes even shady. While long, wordy policies put most laymen to sleep, sleazy salesmen chasing commission leave the impression that it's not about protection but profit. How can you avoid the traps and gaps?

I grew up in insurance, literally. Immersed in the industry from a young age, I grew up to view insurance much differently than most people. I am an insurance evangelist. I believe it is my responsibility to help you eliminate vulnerability by simplifying the process and providing protection solutions. It's my job to help you navigate to a safe harbor. I have little tolerance when I hear the horror stories and I am driven by my own need to put things right, delivering integrity and original intention to people in the form of protection. In the employee benefits space, this translates to helping companies take care of their people.

I wrote this book to help bridge the gap between benefit decision-makers and the technical complexity of the industry. Benefit programmes must change to meet the demands of the new generation employee. The financial crisis that began in 2008 has certainly been a primary catalyst for change. The employee and employer landscape continues to shift; indeed, it has become vastly unrecognizable to anyone who was working prior to the crash.

This shift is really about people and partnerships. Employees now exist in a culture of entitlement and are hungry for a more engaging relationship with their employers. Employers, on the other hand, are well aware of the potential for their top talent to leave them if they don't feel valued and cared for. Companies on a global scale, big and small, are being invited into a deeper experience of the give and get relationship of employment, as employees are demanding employers who are transparent, accountable, and most of all, who create a culture of caring and trust.

Further, employees are now embracing mobility as a competitive advantage in their career pursuits and more and more people seek enticing jobs all around the world. For this reason, employers have to come up with attractive and engaging reasons to encourage their employees to stay. Having a comprehensive benefits package can be an alluring reason to stay with a company. As an employer, building this doesn't have to be a painful process or cost you a fortune to get it right. The value in creating a sustainable and strong employee benefit proposition will pay back in dividends and generate an incredible return on investment, increasing retention of your top talent and driving strong team morale which will elevate your employer brand.

Based on observation, experience and insights during my lifetime in the industry, I have created the Benefits Blueprint. This book is a blend of true stories of insurance nightmares and a how-to guide to avoid the same. The five steps in the Benefits Blueprint are easy to do and, if followed, will launch your company into the brave new world.

The blueprint begins with the necessity of building your HR and Benefits Philosophy. Every company should have one, and you will understand how having this provides a solid foundation for the rest of the steps.

Step two is all about conducting a thorough benefits exercise. Here you will leave no stone unturned as you uncover what your employees need in terms of cover, and how that is best acquired. The time spent in this category will save your company thousands in both dollars and sense. I will share how you save spending in your structure while staying committed to your team's safety and wellbeing.

In step three, I show you how to build the infrastructure to support your Benefits Philosophy and maximize the results of your efforts in the benefits exercise. Again, creative crafting does not have to be a costly or resource-heavy endeavor, and it is achievable whether you are a start-up or a long-running business with hundreds of employees.

Step four in the Benefits Blueprint is possibly the biggest secret weapon you've got. Get this step right and you will master the art of empowering and engaging your workforce. This step will make your employee benefits bulletproof.

Finally, step five is all about maintenance. Reviews at renewal are essential to your strong and sustainable benefits strategy and will ensure that your hard work and efforts will pay back.

Throughout the book, I have provided extra information on a wide range of related topics. You will read about the lay of the land in the insurance world and learn about insider tools of the trade, like benchmarking and profiling. You will understand what flexible benefits really are and be able to determine whether they are the right fit for you and your company.

To me, the future of employment, and the future of insurance, will be built upon a foundation of the partnerships we create. Let this book be a token of the partnership I seek to create with you. There should no longer be a veil of mystery and complexity over how industry insiders create sustainable and successful programmes. I have insights and knowledge to share that will simplify the process of structuring health insurance protection within your total employee benefits proposition. As you build a culture of trust and transparency within your employee population and work in partnership with providers, the more engaged you become with your people. It is my passion for protection – and my responsibility – that drives me to help you navigate to safe harbor in this brave new world.

# Chapter 1

# NAVIGATING FROM NEW YORK TO MY NEW WORLD

"Here," my colleague Cheryl said, presenting me with a shot glass full of vodka. "Take a shot."

It was nine in the morning.

After the second shot, she pushed me out of the office before I could lose my nerve. There was something I had to do.

It was August 2006 and fortified by vodka, I resigned from my marketing role at AIG. As I did, I announced that I was relocating to Asia. My partner had been offered an expatriate package with AIG, and I was following him. We were moving to Singapore. From that day forward, my life changed at the same speed as the financial markets.

The Lion City of Singapore became my home. I planned to spend my early days settling into life in Asia and exploring the region. One of the first tasks on my to-do list was to find travel insurance to cover us for all our adventures. Considering that both my partner and I were from insurance backgrounds, you would think it would have been easy for us to find. It proved to be quite the challenge, however, and a painful one, at that. After a significant search effort, we gave in and decided AIG would have the answer. Even this proved disastrous, however, as we found ourselves on a Canadian-based website. If we, two people in the know on insurance, struggled to find the coverage we needed for a few trips abroad, we could only imagine what the rest of the expatriate world was finding, or not finding.

Living as an unmarried couple in Asia also created unanticipated challenges with insurance. Without any legal marriage status we could not insure our valuables together. No one seemed to be able to help us. There was no one available to talk to or provide a solution for us. Frustrations mounted as the task of securing insurance, something that would take moments to do in the US, became increasingly impossible. Finally, I phoned a fellow American who worked with Chubb Masterpiece and he helped us find the right product. I didn't realize it at the time, but this problem – and the lengths we went to solve it - proved to be a valuable turning point in my professional life.

As we settled in Singapore and my network grew, so did my opportunities. I joined a prominent art gallery. The client base was growing at a rapid pace, and I worked with the owner on re-branding. The gallery's target clientele were expatriates and the high net worth community in Asia. Although I enjoyed my work, the timing was all wrong for me. The financial crisis of 2008 sent people to their financial shelters with all of their disposable income. The news of a looming implosion at AIG hovered around my partner and I at the exact same time I made my exit from the gallery.

It was clear that my next adventure had already been mapped out. Our own early and ongoing frustrations finding insurance while living abroad had been echoed by everyone I met. Wherever and however I met someone, once they knew I had an insurance background, they always shared the same disheartening experience we had in finding the right coverage, or any at all. Some had even given up on their search and risked being without.

Insurance has been all I have ever known. My mother, aunts and cousins, my husband, and myself, we all have careers in insurance. Holidays during my university days were spent interning in Hank Greenberg's AIG. Insurance is in my blood. It was a natural fit for me to be the one to help people through their insurance search, and Expat Insurance was founded.

As the global financial crisis continued, companies began scaling back employee benefit programmes. Expatriate packages were costly and times had changed. Just as I founded Expat Insurance, there was a flood of repatriation and localization offers. Companies needed to crunch their expense lines. It was common knowledge among expatriates that the chances of getting a job upon repatriation to the US or Europe were slim given the economic downturn.

A new breed of expatriate was born and became the norm. Expat Insurance focused on serving the needs of expatriates as private clients.

In the early days of the business, people with employer-sponsored medical insurance benefits would frequently ask me to help them understand their coverage. I found that most companies provided little or no communication about the benefits they offered their employees. Expat Insurance stepped in to educate, engage and advise within the community. I spoke at events and published articles across many of the expatriate organizations and chambers. The goal was to help people understand and become aware about their protection. I would review the benefits they had, give them context about local medical expenses for treatment and talk to them about their needs and expectations so I could provide advice on how to determine the appropriate level of coverage for their family.

I was meeting with a client whom stopped in with an 88-page slide presentation her husband had downloaded from the HR portal at work. I was at the tail end of explaining how her husband's employee benefits programme would respond if her son needed his tonsils removed.

She looked up at me in shock, "Did you say $7,500?"

Her husband worked for a major financial institution in Singapore, so understandably she was surprised to find the medical cover would leave them $7,500 out of pocket if her son had to have a simple procedure.

I explained, "This is not unusual and it's important for you to understand how your benefits will respond if something does happen."

Much calmer, she said, "Thank gosh nothing's happened yet. Is there anything we can do to ensure we don't have to pay if we do need treatment?" I talked her through the top-up options available to complement the family's existing coverage.

After thousands of benefit reviews, it was rarely the limits or coverage that surprised me. It was always the lack of understanding people had for their benefits.

> Companies did not seem to be spending time communicating with their employees, providing information or educating them about the benefits offered.

I often had to instruct clients to go back to HR and ask for a copy of the benefits schedule, letting them know that only then was I able to review their benefits for them. I recall one client continued to seem confused as to why I needed more information, thinking he had given me all that he had received from HR. I let him know what I had didn't tell us whether there were any benefit limits. In this case, he had only given me information listing what was covered and what wasn't, but not how these things were covered. It was very rare to find someone who actually understood their employer-sponsored benefits.

My mission became to educate everyone who called or came through our doors. When people are educated they are empowered. Medical insurance benefits are a means of protection at a time when you need it most. If you understand your coverage, you can make decisions that are right for your needs: if it leaves gaps or has limits, you understand the impact or can top-up with a private policy.

> After all, insurance is a promise that should deliver protection.

Education is about engagement and empowerment and with this comes the peace of mind a benefits programme is designed to offer.

Transitioning from the private client business to employee benefits did not happen by choice, but by force. My phone rang one morning and, after a quick hello, Mark said he needed me to come in to review his firm's benefits.

Mark was COO at Reflect Geophysical, now part of the Otto Marine Group, and was an existing private client of Expat Insurance. We had taken care of his family ever since their arrival in South East Asia. Operating in the oil and gas exploration industry, Reflect have vessels around the globe, including waters off Iran, South America and Russia. Their crew are a highly specialized team and the unique needs of the group were hindering the finance team responsible for managing the insurance policies in place.

The group had grown to over three hundred headcount in just three years, but challenges had struck their recruitment efforts. In addition, retention and turnover were coming into focus as well. Big players in the oil and gas industry offered comprehensive health insurance as part of their employee benefits programme, which Reflect struggled to match with their existing policy structure.

In our meeting, Mark showed me the existing policy benefits. "We need to do better," he said.

To really understand, I asked him to ignore the benefits programme and talk to me about the company's challenges. None of what he shared with me was about benefits. He spoke about morale matters, their competition, feedback from his team and the crew managers. It was about business strategy for the future, where they started and where they wanted to go. Scaling the company could not continue if he didn't fix these problems. Understanding their existing people practices and philosophy helped me understand how they wanted to get where they wanted to go as a business. Only then did we turn to why and how he felt health insurance benefits were part of the problem and begin reviewing the existing benefits structure.

"Mark, this is an exciting project and I definitely think I can help guide you but who can help you roll out and launch the benefits with your team and then manage the programme?"

His response was immediate, "You will. Get in here and sort it out."

I told Mark, "I have to be clear, our expertise is reviewing benefits and aligning coverage to suit the needs of the individual families covered by the programme. We've never taken care of three hundred people all over the world under one programme."

Mark leaned back in his chair. After a moment, he said, "Think of us like one big family. Every one of us has needs and we all want the benefits to take care of us, our wives and children. You'll need to think about every one of the crew just like you focused on each of my family members when you sorted out my private policy. You'll figure it out."

As it turned out, oil and gas was a perfect starting point. Within that industry is a globally mobile workforce with more nationalities than the United Nations. It was an ideal match to our existing client base. The people who made up their team needed coverage to ensure that if they were injured or ill they could get treatment as quickly and smoothly as possible to make their next business trip. Of course, for them, that business trip happened to be their next offshore rotation wherever their vessel was at the time.

That moment marked the beginning of my shift from transforming the thousands of employee benefit reviews I had done, to helping a company structure a health insurance programme to take care of their people so they could carry on with their business. I tailored our service proposition to cater to the group's needs. We worked with the crew managers, operations and finance teams to structure a direct-to-member launch. Our team worked with their team to understand how they interacted with their people. We wanted to speak the corporate language so there was synergy in all our communications. We created a seamless infrastructure to support, resourced by our team as an extension of Reflect's own team. The mission was to work in partnership, using the employee benefits programme as the foundation to get the business back on track.

The rest is history.

# Chapter 2

## CLIMATE CHANGE

"The full package."

Prior to the financial crisis, this is how we used to refer to the remuneration structure that started an expatriate assignment. This phrase meant that you were not a penny out of pocket for virtually anything - rent, car, healthcare, children's education, a home-leave flight for the family in business class, electric and cable bills, air conditioning and heating bills, or just about any other fixed expense. Employee benefit packages took care of it all. You were provided additional compensation if you accepted a role based in a third world country, also known as a hardship posting. With every expense covered, all but your social life and personal travels, salary was savings and life was good.

Specifically for health insurance benefits, employees had the expectation that their employer would provide for all treatment and care required whilst employed with the company. In all areas which may have represented financial vulnerability for the employee and their family, there was little room for disappointment, as this would risk a request to be repatriated and the expense the company had borne to relocate the family for the role. The company took care of everything in an effort to entice you abroad.

The credit crunch ushered in a need for companies to reduce their expense lines in an effort to endure tougher financial times. Employee benefits felt the impact in a lot of firms. Adding to this, unemployment rates across the Western world were at their highest in decades. Companies operating in Asian markets including hardship postings were now sought after for jobs. An increasingly common expatriate story became about the individual or family who relocated to Asia to look for work. This is a grave departure from ten years earlier when companies had to sweeten the deal considerably to encourage people to make the move East.

I interviewed Karen Clifford, former Human Resources Director for South East Asia at Towers Watson. She now owns KC Consulting and offers executive coaching, HR consultancy, leadership development and cultural change support to clients. In terms of the difference between Asia and the rest of the world, Karen pointed out that "There is now a lot of employment in [SE Asia], so unlike Europe and the US, the employees are in more demand than the employers. That has shifted the emphasis, as well."

The remuneration structure for most expatriate assignments of today is a hybrid or local package. In the case of local packages, benefits are a match to those offered to employees hired locally in country, without any additional benefits to accommodate the fact you are living away from your home country. Hybrid packages are a blend between the local package and the more traditional expatriate benefit offering. A hybrid package may include rental, transport or schooling assistance but on average covers only 25-50% of those expenses. The new employee benefit programmes typically include no pension, no savings and no repatriation expenses.

> The financial downturn in the West almost entirely eliminated the need for companies to entice employees abroad with a full-suite employee benefits package.

Health insurance benefits typically fall in line with the new packages on offer across Asia, where the majority of programmes are structured to be competitive locally. While benefits vary widely from country to country, companies generally offer a basic level of hospitalization coverage and a restricted network of local clinics for outpatient care. For most employees, whether or not you're an expatriate, benefits have significant gaps and limitations on coverage. More so if you are an expatriate and local insurance is designed to act in tandem with national healthcare systems available only to local nationals. No longer are all employers providing employees with full-scale benefits for themselves and their families.

When insurance protection programmes are scaled back, employees feel the financial burden when they require treatment. This is often a critical and intimate time. When resources to support the benefit programmes are scaled back, employees and employers both feel the burden. Employees often do not get the responses or answers they need or want, while employers feel the consequential morale impact from both the lack of support made available to the employee, and the shock of the financial burden an employee has experienced.

The landscape has changed. "The complexities of managing a global workforce — addressing external factors affecting the competitiveness of cost structures, sourcing talent and understanding people across cultures — have rendered the work environment unsettling, at best, for both employers and employees. And through this uncertainty, one constant is the pressure to tightly manage costs. Organizations continue to shift some of their increasing cost and risk burden onto employees, while at the same time trying to find a formula to avoid the potential impacts of this strategy on attraction, retention and business performance." (Towers Watson, Global Talent Management and Rewards Study, 2012-2013)

While many companies often focus on mobility as part of their business strategy, people have begun to see themselves as mobile for the same strategic reasons in the employment battleground. Increasingly, people are moving from one company to the next as well as one country to the next, at higher rates than previously experienced. In my interview with Karen Clifford, she commented that along with being more mobile, "[...]people's expectations of what they can achieve in their career have changed [and there is] almost an entitlement culture."

It was similarly observed by Bridget Miller, in the report on HR and Employment Trends for 2015, that: "Turnover is increasing. With the economy growing, unemployment shrinking, and pay rising, employees are in a position where they're not afraid to look for new roles. In past generations, it was uncommon to switch jobs frequently. In the past couple of decades, however, the average number of jobs held during one's lifetime has nearly doubled. With technology making job searching easier, this trend shows no signs of slowing." (HR and Employment Trends for 2015, Bridget Miller)

When it comes to how employees and employers relate, there has been a major paradigm shift over the past decade. This has not just impacted the West or expatriate employees. Increasingly, people have moved away from the standard mentality of considering what benefits their employer provides, to thinking about what benefits they want from their company. "The balance of power in the employer-employee relationship has shifted—making today's employees more like customers or partners than subordinates." (Global Human Capital Trends 2015, Deloitte)

The upheaval of global markets has given birth to a new generation of employee.

"Employees are now like customers; companies have to consider them volunteers, not just workers: As the job market has heated up and new technologies have exploded, power has shifted from the employer to the employee.

Websites like Glassdoor, LinkedIn, Facebook, and others not only increase transparency about a company's workplace; they make it far easier for employees to learn about new job opportunities and gain intelligence about company cultures." (Global Human Capital Trends 2015, Deloitte)

The new generation employee has an increasing preference for choice and a voice when it comes to their benefits. Karen Clifford also reiterated this, when she said, "In the past, you used to interview people, and the focus was around them doing the selling, interviewees making sure they shared all their skills and experience. There is now much more of an even playing field; [but] much more of an even playing field with the employee checking the employer, the culture, and how it is going to benefit them, whether it is going to fit into their lifestyle, the flexibility they want, and/or their career aspirations. There is more of a two-way discussion, rather than a one-way 'sell yourself and we might give you a job' type of a mentality."

Towers Watson's 2015 report on Asia Pacific Benefit Trends notes this change is a preference among employers as well, "Statistics suggest that employers are gradually moving away from a culture of benefits entitlement, and towards encouraging employees to take ownership and control of their benefits." There is an increasing preference for companies to encourage their employees to manage benefits independently and be accountable for their own personal financial protection.

While mobility affords employers and employees a more strategic position, when it comes to people's health, life and retirement plans, concern over the transferability and continuity of coverage tends to increase the desire to independently manage benefits rather than relying on employer-sponsored programmes.

As more and more employees gain independence and take the driver's seat when it comes to their protection, understanding their benefits and how their families would be covered in the instance of an accident, illness or death is essential.

In their 2014 Global Benefit Attitudes survey, Towers Watson found that, "... employees view benefits such as retirement and health as an important reason to work for or stay with their current employer." Employers are either not listening or unsure how to respond appropriately to this dramatic shift in people's mindsets because, contrary to this sentiment, Towers Watson also reported that currently, "... only 16% say that employees value their benefits highly." Employers have to decide how to support this change and take action.

Turnover and poor retention rates are costly for employers and the statistics show grave concern for the costs companies may bear if "86% of employees are already looking for work outside their current occupations and nearly one third of employers expect workers to job hop." (10 Workplace Trends for 2015, Forbes, Dan Schawbel)

In order to attract and retain top talent in their industry, companies will need to shift their strategies to offer benefits better aligned to globally-minded and highly mobile talent while continuing to focus on cost-containment and sustainability of a benefits programme. "A highly competitive global talent market has shifted power into the hands of employees, forcing HR to redesign programmes in the face of a much more demanding workforce." (Global Human Capital Trends 2015, Deloitte) As companies expand overseas, HR leaders and benefit decision-makers need to create their benefit structures locally while keeping a global focus due to the new mobility demands of employers and employees alike. "For human resources (HR) organizations, this new world requires bold and innovative thinking. It challenges our existing people practices."

For companies with a diverse and globally mobile workforce which includes a blended workforce of locals and foreigners in country, challenges arise in determining the structure of an appropriate protection programme. Diversity in an employee population brings differing perspectives and expectations when it comes to protection, remuneration and benefits. It's critical for employers to understand each of these perspectives and appreciate the view from every angle. For companies with a solely local workforce, there are far fewer challenges. Employers can rely on an understanding of the benefits afforded by a national healthcare system. Employers are also guided by statutory requirements for coverage, and can benchmark to establish the expectation of their employees when it comes to benefits.

If we focus our attention on how a particular company structures a balanced remuneration package which may include any combination of salary and non-salaried benefits, we can segment the order of importance for insurance protection benefits. We then look to establish whether or not this order of importance is a true reflection of what the company wants employees to understand about working for them.

"The most important part of the insurance programme is to ensure employees are well looked after if they are ill or have an accident." This is one of the most common replies I hear when I ask about the purpose and intention of a company's benefit programme. My immediate response is to dig deeper and figure out what we mean by "well looked after."

> Understanding a company's relationship with their employee population is a critical part of structuring a benefits programme which creates positive morale impact.

By creating a remuneration package which provides active remuneration as well as protection aligned with a company's view of how they want to look after their employees, you have a solid foundation when you communicate the benefit programme as you have anticipated expectations and feel strongly about crafting the message to the team accordingly.

There is no single response or protection solution that can answer the needs of everyone in your workforce. As we enter this new and more complex age of employment as partnership, some companies will strike the right balance with their benefit programmes while others will make changes that provide no positive impact or, worse, get it wrong, costing time, money and reputation. When a company considers all the perspectives - a diverse workforce, from management to the cleaner, a multi-national team, local statutory requirements, internal stakeholders including HR, finance and line managers -- it can be a minefield to understand what everyone needs, feels and wants from a benefits programme.

For seasoned HR leaders it may seem like my first move is for amateurs. Let's go back to basics and remind ourselves of the construct of the phrase, "employee benefits." The definition of "benefit":

- Something that is advantageous or good;
- A payment or gift, as one made to help someone or given by an employer;
- Archaic: an act of kindness.

We need to start by reminding ourselves that the inherent principal behind benefits is providing the employee, your people, with something advantageous or good, first and foremost. The benefit is also payment for work or service but with the express purpose of helping.

Employee benefits may also be called benefits-in-kind or perks and can include a variety of non-wage related compensation provided to employees in addition to their normal wages or salary. Examples of these benefits include:

housing, group insurance (health, dental, life, travel, accident), disability income protection, retirement benefits, daycare, tuition or education reimbursement, sick leave, vacation, transportation, social security, profit sharing, memberships, and other specialized or flexible benefits.

The purpose of employee benefits is to increase the economic security of staff members, and in doing so, positively impact and improve retention across an organization. It is part of the total package where a company rewards people fairly, equitably and consistently in accordance with their value to the organization. By defining this basic principal, we also remind ourselves of the benefits for the employer: increased retention, positive impact when attracting talent and a strong corporate culture of caring for your people.

So how do you develop a benefits programmeme that will create value for this new generation employee and subsequently create value for the organization? The new climate forces us to throw away the old playbook and deliver more innovative solutions. The answer to this question lies in the company taking the lead while all partners within the value chain take responsibility. Traditional employee benefit practices are undergoing radical change. There is both challenge and opportunity to be found in creating employee benefits programmes that speak to an ever-evolving world.

## Section 2

# THE BENEFITS BLUEPRINT

# Chapter 3

# TICK BOX TANGO

The five steps of the Benefits Blueprint were really born out of the need I identified with every new client that came through our doors. Insurance is a complex and technical industry. Given my lifetime of experience with it, I knew I could offer help to people trying to navigate their way to the promise of protection.

Before we get started on the steps to creating bullet-proof benefits, there are a few stories I want to share that illustrate and emphasize the need to have a strategy and a plan when it comes to coverage. These stories are all real life examples of what can happen; perhaps one of them might have been true for you.

It is all too easy with insurance to buy based on the cost alone. I consider this buying without purpose. When we buy insurance without really understanding what we're getting into, selecting coverage by price rather than taking the time to determine whether what we're buying is really what we need, we are setting ourselves up for trouble. I see this often with clients who play what I call "Tick Box Tango."

There was a tick box and Matt chose the most expensive option. He assumed off-the-shelf plans for SMEs were designed and developed to ensure a price point for even the smallest business and that the highest level would offer FULL coverage.

In the early days of a start-up, there's excitement and energy, and then there's insurance. Advertisements of package programmes designed for small businesses often have alluring brochures. One side of the page describes two different small businesses and the insurance company's unique selling points. The other side outlines five different levels of coverage with a heading that states: "Special solutions for you… choose from the following according to your requirements." The simplicity of a tick box makes buying quick and easy: job done with one quick tick.

But how do you decide which box to tick? The box on the right shows smaller costs, but a lot of caveats. Words fill the lines where benefits should be. The box on the left has less words and therefore more benefits, right? Because the premium is triple the one to the right it offers more coverage, right? So Matt ticked the box.

It works in both directions. Matt could have chosen Plan C because he wanted to save money. Or Plan A, because it was the most expensive and therefore likely the most coverage. Playing tick box tango this way, does he go with

Plan B and take the cost cut? Or does he go with Plan A? He dances back and forth, the torturous tango.

It is generally believed that the most expensive plan is going to be better.

> Most insurance companies do not want to customize benefits for small companies.

To them, it's too much administration and too much fuss to tailor for smaller firms (between five to fifty employees), so they create products which can be purchased off-the-shelf. They advertise choice, "Choose Plan A, B, C, D or E," or "Plan 1, 2, 3, 4 or 5."

They scale benefits from a low price point all the way up to a higher level price point, and the thought process that goes on in a lot of people's minds is, *The most expensive option will provide fully covered, comprehensive benefits and take care of everything.* They're staring at a piece of paper with no context. They're in a small firm, so they go to HR – if there even is an HR, beyond an office manager – and they ask, "Do you understand this?" But sometimes people don't want to admit that they themselves, as decision-makers, don't understand what they're doing. There's a fear of not wanting to go to someone else and ask, "Do you understand what these benefits are?"

So they see the piece of paper, they choose the most expensive one or the option in the middle, and they figure if an insurance company put a higher price point on this one, it must be good, it must be the best. *I'll just choose that one and I'm sure we'll be fine.*

Paul is a Brit and was hired as Managing Director of the boutique recruitment firm Matt started in Singapore. While working there, Paul had a heart attack. He was admitted to hospital, and needed a pacemaker. While the costs of treatment were paid in full, the device itself became problematic for the company. Only $5,000 was payable under the plan they had ticked. The total cost of the device was $15,000, leaving $10,000 outside the scope of the benefits Matt elected in the company's Tick Box Tango. To pay or not to pay?

Even if he decides, from an HR perspective, they are going to treat everyone the same, regardless of nationality, regardless of whether they are a local or a foreigner, the majority of the programmes designed by local insurance companies that show up as an option in the tick boxes are designed with local nationals in mind. They are designed, written and priced for the local market. Shelf solutions are developed based on the majority. The majority in Singapore is five million, foreigners represent only a fraction of that total market size. So with a diverse workforce, why would you dance this tick box tango between five programmes when none of them have been designed with your company profile in mind? You are sure to twirl into turbulence. What's the solution?

What if there was no extra cost to you receiving a tailored solution? What if there was no extra cost to you reviewing plan A from one insurer and plan D from another? What if we put them next to each other, and then I give you context and advice to make the right choice for your group?

It is my goal to help you have a clearer understanding of just what you're choosing when you are faced with the tick box tango. The following chapters discuss the five steps in the Benefits Blueprint. When your steps are choreographed, you will learn there are far more options than the tick boxes made available to you in the brochure.

# Chapter 4

# STEP 1:
# HR AND BENEFITS PHILOSOPHY

The first step in the Benefits Blueprint is to understand your company's HR and Benefits Philosophy. Established companies with a strong corporate culture and leadership team tend to have a clearly defined Benefits Philosophy. You can identify this straight away if the philosophy is quickly and easily articulated by everyone in the organization. The philosophy runs like a vein through your organization, reaching beyond HR leaders and through to management and employees alike.

The latest buzz phrase in the HR community is "employee value proposition," or EVP. The phrase represents a desire for employers and talent alike to truly understand the employment deal, or the "give" and "get". EVP is viewed from an employee-centric approach and is closely related to employer branding or an employer brand proposition.

It helps answer the question: why is the total work experience at your organization superior to that of your competitor? The EVP encourages employers and employees alike to shift the focus off of compensation as the sole and primary offer, at every stage of the employment partnership. While your EVP helps you develop your HR and Benefits Philosophy, the two are not to be confused. EVP is far larger than benefits alone.

> Your people policies, processes and programmes all help demonstrate your organization's commitment to your talent.

Whether it is employee growth, development, recognition, community impact, achieving clarity of your EVP will help guide the HR and Benefits Philosophy.

While fast growth start-ups often have a strong corporate culture, they often miss the importance of defining a benefits strategy in the early days of the business. Regardless of the size of your company, protection and a benefits strategy is key. Here's a story to illustrate why.

## A Dog Bit My Face

James is an innovator in the food and beverage space. He had come into the office to meet me. James had hired Dave, a young, single expatriate, to manage a new restaurant and bar concept he had launched. Dave arrived in Singapore without any medical coverage as the employment contract he had signed included a commitment to the offer of medical insurance benefits.

Unbeknownst to Dave, there was no cover purchased for him. James had not yet relocated himself, and was managing the operation from overseas. Business came first and benefits would be an afterthought. Dave, the young expat employee, never thought twice to ask and was counting on the fact that he would be taken care of should anything happen.

Sure enough, something did happen. Dave had a freak accident when he was bitten in the face by a dog. He was checked into a hospital and needed to undergo a minor face reconstruction to rebuild the jaw bone and cheek. The bills racked up immediately following the accident, coming to a total of $51,000 in the first three days. Dave was handed the bill when he checked out of the hospital and managed to settle the entire cost on a credit card, well, more like five different credit cards. Afterward, Dave contacted James to find out what to do and where to send all of the receipts for his reimbursement. It was then that James had to share that there was no cover in place.

When I sat down in the meeting, James wanted to talk through the situation to see if we could do anything to help him with the bills. I explained that insurance is about protection for the unexpected, it's not designed to be, nor can it be, purchased after the fact to cover existing expenses. James needed to determine how to handle the costs and manage Dave's expectations as to how he would be able to respond without the benefits afforded by an insurance programme.

What Dave expected was for his bills to be taken care of for the accident. That was consistent with what would have been provided if this kind of an accident had happened in his home country. Dave quoted his contract and referenced the promise of health insurance benefits. The expectation of coverage was clear and could not be challenged.

All James could do was reiterate that there was no cover- er. The new business operation didn't even have $51,000 in the bank to write the check and pay. The business would have to either loan from its overseas entity to pay this bill or respond by telling Dave that he was not covered.

After James walked through our door, the main pur- pose was to determine how it would have been covered if he had purchased insurance for the employees before the accident. Then he would be able to make a decision around what to do next. By using the coverage design to establish how the bills would or would not have been covered were there a programme in place, James was hoping to use this to guide a reasonable response and create credibility given the situation at hand. I explained that he was too narrowly focused, it was not about coverage alone.

> Part of having benefits is educating your employees and your workforce to understand what their coverage is.

This way, they can determine for themselves wheth- er coverage is sufficient or whether it may leave them fi- nancially vulnerable. If it does, they have the opportunity to top-up their cover and put whatever cover they feel is personally appropriate in place. They use the employee benefits cover as the baseline and then they can build on that if it alone is not suitable to their needs.

But let's get back to the $51,000 bill. James had to dig deep and make an ethical call as to how to respond. Was he was prepared to pay or not, and on what basis would he decide? Writing the check meant loaning from one of the company's overseas entities before business barely even began in Singapore. Such a big bill at the beginning was certainly going to impact business strategy.

What I shared with James was the foundation and basis of benefits; they are provided to strengthen the economic security of your employees. Because there had been no conversation, no education, no benefits at all that provided a foundation for James' dog-bitten employee, I encouraged him to take responsibility for the lack of action. He needed to make this decision on the basis of how he valued Dave and the rest of his team. I wanted him to appreciate that the precedent set by the major decision made around this particular situation would clearly impact the company and all of its employees, not just the one with the bitten face and big bill. It had the potential to impact the company's reputation moving forward. If it all went wrong and went viral on social media or, even worse, became a legal matter, the bill had the potential to be far larger than the existing $51,000 tab. The impact would be much greater than financial burden alone.

Even companies with a programme in place and a clearly defined Benefits Philosophy can experience challenges such as this. This is because there is often discontinuity between how the company feels about the provision of benefits and the way the employees view the benefits being provided. "Surprisingly few companies (22%) take their employees' views into account to a great extent when determining which benefits to offer... Taking into account employee opinion is essential to creating an effective benefits programme that has relevance across a multigenerational and diverse workforce." (2015 Asia Pacific Benefit Trends, Towers Watson)

If you are a fast growth start-up, or a satellite and subsidiary office set-up, you may be focusing on incentivized remuneration structures which may or may not include an emphasis on protection benefits. You may have an incredibly strong corporate culture which is energy rich but, in my experience, many firms with small numbers allow employees to take protection into their own hands in the early days, much to their detriment. This shifts the responsibility to the employee and alleviates the need for the company to take action. But this direction leads us down a spiralling path as there is not a clear focus on creating a benefit strategy. It can be a costly mistake, as it often takes time and money to create and action a new and clear direction later as the business scales and employee numbers grow. "Particularly as organizations grow, or as their workforces mature, the needs of their employees will evolve." (2015 Asia Pacific Benefit Trends, Towers Watson)

## Reap The Rewards With Forward-Thinking

When a technology services firm set-up operations in Singapore they started with two senior management team members on the ground. Like most other companies, their original focus was about getting coverage in place quickly so they could focus their attention on business strategy, growth plans and sales.

When I met with the CFO from their Australian office, I took the opportunity to share with him the challenges many other companies have if they haphazardly throw coverage together in the early days. Once they grow to a size where a more formalized benefits structure for the group offers cost and coverage benefits as well as seamless administration, consolidation becomes nearly impossible without costing money, time and headaches. Not to mention the morale management required when you change people's benefits and policies. If they go forth down this path initially, by the time a company reaches ten to thirty employees, they need to stop and recalibrate their response to benefits in order to avoid the serious challenges that continued growth often presents with no clear benefits direction.

Some of these challenges include the drain on resources when someone manages individual policies which expire throughout the course of a year. Companies face higher costs when purchasing individual policies, as they are unable to leverage group buying power and their economy of scale which offer increased benefits at reduced costs. In addition, there is also the potential for a higher burden of cost if an employee should leave the company.

> If the company has reimbursed the premium for the private policies upfront and the policy is issued to the employee directly, then the company will potentially be unable to recover the cost for the pro-rated time after the employee leaves the company.

There is an inherent lack of control when policies are issued to the individual rather than the company. Another challenge is the fact that employees may also have varying levels of coverage with different insurance companies when managed independently, so there is no synergy in the benefits being provided or reimbursed by the company. One employee may have full coverage with no out of pocket costs while another employee purchased a plan covering only accidents and emergencies and providing no outpatient benefits.

I worked with this tech services firm to identify the coverage required to meet their business needs, not for the business they were at the time but for the business they planned to be over the next twelve to twenty-four months. Starting with the programme needed to be able to deliver due to the demands of the business and the team in the long-term allowed us to open the discussion about the kind of employer they needed to become to successfully reach their business goals. I helped them imagine what the team will need, want and expect. From this point, we could then establish the foundation of their programme design based on HR and benefit philosophy. They reaped the rewards of their time spent in this initial phase within the first five months of operations. The programme scaled seamlessly as the team grew from two to twelve across three countries.

It's easy to see there is big benefit and return on investment in determining early on how a company wants to respond to employee's protection needs. Developing a programme structure for two members is easier said than done but creative product design and forward thinking insurance companies help you accomplish the job. The company had plans and budget to grow from two to fifty plus in less than twelve months, so I worked with them to define their benefit philosophy at the beginning and set them on a path which avoided recalibrating as they grow the business.

Common questions you should ask to better define your HR and Benefits Philosophy:

- Do you want employees to be fully covered in the event of an accident or illness, leaving them with no out of pocket expenses for treatment and care?

- Are you comfortable with the employee having to contribute to their treatment costs? If yes, how much employee contribution is a comfortable amount?

- What level of privacy of care are we offering: public or private? Single room or warded accommodation?

- In the instance of critical illness or cancer, what is the company response to the level of protection that should be provided?
- Would your employees seek treatment locally or overseas in the event of a serious condition or procedure? If you have team members whom are not resident in their home countries, would you want them to be able to choose to travel back to home country for treatment or would the expectation be to receive treatment in their local country of employment?
- Is there an expectation that employees have their own private medical insurance already or will have to purchase a policy to top-up the employee benefits you will provide?
- Are we looking to cover all employees in the same way or do we want to differentiate between categories of employees? On what basis do we design the categories?
- Are we extending protection to employees alone or also to their families?

We are not necessarily looking for specific and direct answers to these questions. Rather, we are working toward using this line of questioning to get to the heart of the general HR response to people and benefits. Open-ended questions tend to provide immediate insight into the view of how important insurance benefits are within the context of the company's culture. If protection when an employee is ill is important, but health and life insurance rank low on the priority list, we need to stop and align coverage to culture. This builds your foundation for a protection and programme philosophy and helps you move with confidence to the next step of the process.

When business strategy or needs change, understanding the HR and Benefits Philosophy helps align – or realign - new benefits with the desired outcome of how we want the programme to resonate and be viewed by the employee population. Indeed, the best HR and Benefits Philosophy will be one that will help you remain flexible and agile in the continuing uncertainty of a dramatically changing global marketplace.

## Cost Savings Come With Clarity

Take the example of another technology firm who create compelling digital solutions for their clients. At the start, we took care of Cole, one of the entrepreneurs in the early days of the business. Within months of his relocation from Australia to Singapore he had set up business and the firm had grown instantly with multiple acquisitions. The company now had a core senior management team and a diverse workforce across ten offices in six countries which required integration.

Each of the firms that were acquired had their own coverage and maintained their policies separately after the acquisition. While the businesses were now merged and consolidating under one strategic direction, the Benefits

Philosophy and design of each of the firms needed to be considered prior to consolidation. While Cole was immediately responsive to a consolidated approach across countries and across the region given their continued growth trajectory, he also wanted to create synergy post-acquisition and leverage the ability to cost contain with the much larger group size. Thus it was critical to take time to understand and appreciate the Benefits Philosophy and culture within each of the companies pre-acquisition. This would also aid our communication and engagement initiatives later on in the process (more on this in Step 4).

First, we mapped out all the active protection policies across the companies. Then, we turned our focus on clearly defining the new HR and Benefits Philosophy for the future of their rapidly growing firm. Within two workshop sessions we were able to better understand the order of importance of protection in relation to the total remuneration package and also how the company wanted to respond to employees across the newly merged firms. Using the new philosophy, we began the consolidation starting with the nearest expiry date, renegotiating the benefits and premium to match the new benefits structure.

> There are major advantages in determining how a company wants to respond to employee's protection needs in the early days of structuring a benefits programme.

This often seems to be overlooked. We save time, money and mistakes in programme structure when we truly understand the HR and Benefits Philosophy. Some clients were led by cost or budget, while others are unsure about how they ended up with what they have in place. Maybe these leaders joined the company after the policies were put in place and never asked questions of their predecessor so there is disconnection between the purpose and programme in place. The majority of clients are unclear about the reasons they offer what they offer to their people as part of the employee benefits programme.

To gain clarity, you need to understand your corporate culture and know your HR responses in exceptional situations. This includes being clear on the view of the employer and employee landscape within the firm itself, expectations of all parties and the current and desired morale of the team when it comes to their benefits. Often we find the current morale is not the same as the desired. An effective health and wellness programme must be targeted and relevant to your people. In addition, determine whether there is a precedent set or guidelines for the company response to exceptional cases. Finally, determine the desired outcome of the total benefits programme.

The bottom line is this: a company, regardless of its size, needs to have a benefits plan in place or at the very least, be able to offer protection which fulfils their commitments to their employees. Whether your company has eight or eight thousand people, being prepared for dog bites - among other scenarios - is essential. When you are designing benefits, think to the future. A company that truly understands the basis of their benefits and creates a culture of trust with their people will always stand out from the crowd when attracting talent in today's competitive global job market.

# Chapter 5

# HR AND BENEFITS PHILOSOPHY: HOW TO AVOID THE BABY BLUES

Never underestimate the impact of HR responses in any situation. The best HR answers are creative, highly attuned to company culture, and get to the heart of the matter, particularly in exceptional situations. In my interview with Stephanie Nash during her time as Vice President Human Resources for Allergan in Asia Pacific (she is now Chief People Officer at Redmart), she spoke of the need for companies and HR leaders to build "HR guardrails". The guardrails are developed to guide goodwill of the company and act as a defence for company decisions in exceptional situations. These HR guardrails help define your HR and Benefits Philosophy. You need to know, how far do you go? Where and when do you stop? This sets a precedent and contributes to a culture of wellbeing within the firm, for leaders and their teams alike.

The next two chapters share stories that highlight the value of a well-crafted HR and Benefits Philosophy and how it serves as a culturally consistent response to employees in extraordinary circumstances.

Michael and Lindsay were a couple in need of help. They found Expat Insurance, and came in to share their situation with me. This lovely couple had been relying on their employee benefits coverage alone and had not really looked into the level of protection it provided them. They had just welcomed a new baby to the world. In the early moments immediately following birth, their pediatrician recognized the little one had an underdeveloped trachea. With little time to act, a neonatal surgeon had to open up the trachea, otherwise the baby would be at risk of severe breathing troubles. The medical bills mounted and at the time of discharge, Mike was handed a hefty bill for $30,000. Mike responded to the receptionist by explaining their insurance was covering the cost. With a nervous and cautious gulp, she replied that she had already contacted the insurance company about the unplanned surgery and that she had been informed it wasn't covered. The insurer had told her to inform Michael to settle the additional bills for the baby's care before they left the hospital.

Michael and Lindsay were completely distressed. They had already been through a rollercoaster of emotions over the last few days. One of the most overwhelming experiences of their lives, welcoming a baby to the world, had been immediately followed by trauma, fear, and stress over the urgent care their newborn needed. This terror had been quickly relieved by the success of the unplanned surgery and knowing the baby was going to be okay. The stress returned as they were unexpectedly hit with a $30,000 bill to pay.

Michael returned to work with Lindsay still in hospital, looking after the baby. He approached HR for an explanation, bringing with him the $30,000 bill, along with the expectation of a positive response to his request for reimbursement.

> It is in these moments that HR leaders, managers and benefit administrators have an opportunity to either make or break morale, based on their response.

If you say, "Sorry, if it's not covered by the insurance, we don't take care of it," Michael is clearly going to walk out the door damaged, potentially going to share this response with all of his colleagues or worse, a much larger community. Further, consider how this may impact his confidence and loyalty in the company. If his morale plummets, his investment and desire to continue to drive business forward are going to be severely affected. This can have disastrous impact in both the short-term and long-term for employee and employer alike.

Having a clear understanding of the "HR guardrails" in place allows for the response in situations like these to be communicated in a consistent way, and in direct alignment with your HR and Benefits Philosophy. When your "HR guardrails" are required, employees should be able to anticipate the message before it is even delivered. If "HR guardrails" are established and relied upon, the leader or manager delivering the response has the opportunity to focus not on the reply itself but on the person instead. This allows a company to engage empathy and understanding. The outcome is that morale will command the attention of the moment.

How do you as a leader establish "HR guardrails"? When you understand what's covered and what's not, you are forced to answer the question: what happens when we have someone whom is not covered for something? When your leaders are clear on the compromises which were made to mitigate premiums, answer the needs of the majority and contain costs, you can be much more proactive in your employee engagement in the event that extraordinary circumstances command the company's attention.

After acting as an intermediary to assist Michael and Lindsay, and the company in this case, I came to understand that the company only covered routine newborn care following birth. They had been told coverage for complications was costly and it was therefore not included in the employee benefits programme. The company had calculated this risk. What they had not done was consider the consequences.

Now imagine if instead the employer had used education as a tool in their engagement initiatives so instead of being in a reactive position, they were able to be proactive and Michael could anticipate any response before requesting it.

If employees understand the benefits you are providing, you can engage your "HR guardrails" far less. It also lends to understanding and acceptance within your workforce when you do have to respond. We worked together with the company to establish whether there was any leeway and flexibility which might lend to a contribution to the costs Michael's case. We collaborated on a compromise and focused on the commitment between both employee and employee to better understand their partnership when it comes to protection.

> Communicating coverage is the key to creating a transparent and consistent culture.

Creating "HR guardrails" allow you to do the work in advance and ensure the response is in line with the HR and Benefits Philosophy as well as the corporate culture of the company. Having a strong HR and Benefits Philosophy creates your armor so that when you have to engage your guardrails the response is impenetrable and the impact is positive. This is why step one in the blueprint is essential.

# Chapter 6

## STEP 2:
## THE BENEFITS EXERCISE

Whether you already have a programme in place or you operate a self-insurance scheme, the next step is to complete a detailed review of what exists. You need to look at every aspect of the programme including your benefit structure, coverage limits, terms and conditions, underwriting, administration and claims procedures. Understanding what is already in place and whether or not a company and their employees are happy is critical. This is the time to also review all of the employee feedback received or solicited. When you review what you already have in place this is your opportunity to:

- Ask questions about why a benefit is included or excluded from coverage
- Review the terms and conditions of coverage
- Uncover gaps of which you may be unaware

- Request employee feedback, including people and their managers
- Open productive discussion which engages all the stakeholders: HR, leadership and management teams
- Identify benefit duplication between two policies which may be adding to your benefits spend without providing any value
- Analyse the benefit spend ratios across all lines of protection, whether it's health, life, disability, retirement, travel or accident insurance.

I hope you find this next fact shocking: "Regionally, over one fifth (22%) of employers do not know how much they're spending on benefits, a nudge up from 2013 when 18% said the same. This suggests that companies are struggling with benefits governance, juggling multiple systems, vendors and administrative platforms." (2015 Asia Pacific Benefit Trends, Towers Watson) I hear companies speak so often about the need to reduce spend and minimize expense lines, but almost a quarter of the companies across Asia Pacific do not understand their benefits spend at all. You need to take time to understand your existing financial commitments to benefits. Doing this creates an opportunity to dramatically increase your ability to respond to the needs and demands of your employee population. This helps you allocate, or re-allocate, spend according to the priorities set-out in the first step when you established your HR and Benefits Philosophy.

When I guide clients through the Benefits Exercise, whether they have had a programme in place for two years or twenty-two years, they always find this part of the process the most enlightening. Time and time again I have engaged in the Benefits Exercise with companies only to discover that they did not understand what the programme provided to employees in any meaningful way. The value of a Benefits Exercise offers total transparency for everyone involved in the process. This removes complexity and helps you simplify. If you do not understand the why behind the benefit structure and premium spend the programme will appear disconnected, disengaged and awkward. In this chapter, I will explain that beyond conducting the Benefits Exercise, there are all kinds of insider tools that come into play. Knowing how to use these tools can be very helpful during the exercise. A layman's glossary provides more detail in Section 3, Tools of the Trade.

One of the results of a Benefits Exercise is that it allows you to see where your money is going when it comes to insurance protection. It is important to pay attention to exactly what benefits are driving cost within your programme and understand what benefits you think you are getting or offering to your employees. I will share the story of an established international school whom had been buying policies direct with a few insurance companies for more than fifteen years. When I worked with them to conduct a Benefits Exercise, we identified a few major issues. Some of these issues were known already to be causing concern and some of the issues were highlighted for the first time during this stage of the process.

## Paid Up With No Protection

Employees were not covered for pre-existing medical conditions, neither at the start of employment nor during their course of employment. No matter how minor, major or chronic, all pre-existing medical conditions were excluded. This brought many challenges, both in the upfront recruitment and package negotiations and in their employee engagement initiatives, as it created discontinuity between their desire to protect and the existing programme design. They understood, for example, that an employee with a high cholesterol diagnosis would have to pay out of pocket for their ongoing follow-up consultations and also for their medication. But they had not yet considered the broader implications of this element of coverage. What if that employee had a heart attack or stroke which may be attributed to their high cholesterol and there was no coverage under the programme? What was the HR response to the employee going to be in this situation? They were unprepared and had no "HR guardrails" in place for just such a scenario, because they were unaware this situation was even a possibility as they had not understood the underwriting implications in this way.

Unexpected exclusions were also a problem for the school when certain situations cropped up within their population. Take allergies, for instance. No one ever recognized there was an exclusion in the policy until one of the children on the programme was diagnosed with a peanut allergy. When the teacher inquired about coverage in the case of their child having an allergic attack, HR learned from the insurer that this was outside the scope of the policy based on the exclusion. The school was then left to make a decision as to how they would respond. Should they pay for the medical treatment the child required or would the burden of these expenses be on the employee? What would the costs be if there was an attack? Did they have an obligation to provide this coverage? What was the morale impact for the teacher if they confirmed the child had wasn't covered? The questions helped provide a clear answer, they were altogether uncomfortable with the exclusion that had been uncovered.

The school took class trips where a total of between 25-60 students would be abroad together with a small group of teachers and parent volunteers. In the existing programme structure, they would approach the insurance company to issue a single-trip travel policy for each trip, as and when required. After eight years of purchasing policies this way, I became involved and took over the single-trip coverage request pending. Upon a policy wording review, I uncovered there was no coverage for medical treatment for students under the age of eighteen. This was true not just for the upcoming trip but also true of all the prior trips as well. I was so shocked when I initially discovered this that I reached out to ask the insurer to confirm this was the case. I had to ask the underwriter to repeat his response three times just to be sure I had heard correctly. I pressed further, "You mean to say you charged them for coverage for eight years and if there would have been a claim or evacuation, you would have declined it because you were selling them a policy that didn't cover 95% of the travelers: the students?" Indeed he confirmed that each year they had been selling the school two to three single-trip travel policies for their class trips with all their students, but that there was no cover for medical expenses for any of the students during these trips. I was flabbergasted. The school really had paid up for eight years, and yet coverage was not suited to purpose. They were paid up with no protection.

This is a dramatic example of the industry at its worst, customer loyalty and complacency gone wrong.

> The school had paid thousands in premiums to the same insurer for years, but had no protection, and the insurer was claiming no responsibility.

Imagine if anything had happened to the children on those trips abroad. Fortunately for the school, they had no earth-shattering moments which required decision-making that broke the morale machine entirely. But it was only a matter of time. We were able to work together to fix the programme structure which provided continuity between HR and Benefits Philosophy and the coverage. Needless to say, they elected to change the way they purchased that year.

If you have no current coverage in place, you should review a detailed health insurance benefit schedule and use this as your guide for the exercise. This will prompt the questions you need to be asking about which benefits, at what limits and why. Doing this will also help you gain a better understanding of the company's needs to create a starting point or baseline for the new programme structure. Understanding the benefits that make up the programme is important as you can ensure benefit spend is being optimized to suit your company's needs from a price perspective.

Go through this exercise of reviewing a benefits table twice. In the first round of the review, use a worksheet and create your ideal benefit table. In round two, review the table again but this time with a focus on the price impact of each of the benefit lines. This will help keep you in check at the early stages of structuring the programme to avoid a time-consuming reworking of the programme benefits later on. If you forget about price drivers now, you may find yourself removing a benefit later to bring the cost back in line with your budget. If you are forced to make these decisions quickly later on, you may make dramatic changes without allowing you and your team to consider the impact of the change, however minor. This may cost you more than the benefit you just removed. During the Benefits Exercise you are trying to focus on transparency and alignment with your HR and Benefits Philosophy. Always come back to your HR and Benefits Philosophy to validate your decision-making. That is the foundation on which you build your benefits.

Whether or not coverage is already in place, the Benefits Exercise should be your comprehensive fact find, conducted with the aim of establishing a full needs analysis of the company and your employee population. Round two provides the double check to ensure it is affordable to answer the needs identified in a specific way. If you do have an existing programme, here's where I recommend you get started.

Review what I refer to as "the good, the bad and the ugly" of the existing programme. This is a great place to begin, as it provides a high-level snapshot when you discuss company and employee views. It will also highlight concerns within the current coverage. The focus then becomes maintaining the good while fleshing out the bad and the ugly to determine how the issues or coverage highlighted can be addressed or fixed to create positive impact. There are times when the good can be tweaked to fix the bad or the ugly without generating a negative response from employees.

Here is another story to illustrate how this is possible once your corporate culture and HR and Benefits Philosophy are clearly defined.

## Solid Foundations Provide Freedom Of Choice

We were at the step of renewal review with an innovative mobile technology firm (we discuss renewal reviews in-depth in Chapter 11). I had structured their original programme a few years prior when they were a tech start-up. Each year the company had grown and employee feedback about the restriction of the outpatient clinic network grew at the same scale as the company. The firm's HR and

Benefits Philosophy was clearly defined and it was important for them to consider whether they could afford to move away from this feature within the programme design. During discussions with them we decided together the best approach was to conduct an employee survey wherein we polled employees for their consensus. They were given a choice: would you opt for outpatient benefits with no cap to the coverage but you're require you to stay within the network? Or would you opt for outpatient benefits with a limit to enjoy the freedom of choice to elect which doctors you can visit for treatment?

The overwhelming majority of employees opted for the first choice which provided unlimited benefits within a restricted network. The response was simple: no change was required to the benefits programme. The following year, at renewal review a poll proved employees were happier with the benefits than they had been in previous years. They had been offered a voice and that proved more valuable than a change in their programme. Remember, the goal of the blueprint is to answer new and different demands from your people power in this dynamic employment landscape.

> Rewriting the playbook for HR leaders means creating innovative ways to engage and empower your people.

Think outside the box about how you can achieve this.

Focus groups or anonymous surveys, whether you are getting the perspective from decision-makers and HR leaders or the entire employee population, provide substantial insight at this stage of the process. Employers that "take employee insights into account when determining which benefits to offer see higher value in their benefit programmes." (2015 Asia Pacific Benefit Trends, Towers Watson).

As part of the Benefits Exercise you can also explore whether a tiered programme solution, which responds differently to employee needs or categories of people, is a better fit than a one-benefits-for-all structure. Again, guided by your HR and Benefits Philosophy, the answer to programme structure in this regard should be a reasonably simple response which is agreed by all stakeholders early on. For companies that have an immediate, gut response for all employees to be treated alike, you need to focus on how to achieve a balance of benefits which will meet the expectations of the majority.

Common reasons to consider a tiered solution which provides varied benefits for different categories of employees may be based on the following:

- How an employee is contracted
- Whether an employee is a local or a foreigner in the country of employment (and whether or not they gain any national healthcare benefits)
- The employee's level of seniority within the firm.

With a variety of benefit tiers, companies are able to be agile in how they respond to the diversity among their workforce. In addition, a tiered solution may also answer an increasing need for companies to respond to different generations of employees. For example, a Gen X-er may want more comprehensive coverage for critical and chronic illness when a Gen Y-er may want pregnancy or maternity insurance for themselves or their wives as they consider growing their family.

> Whether a tiered programme or a one-benefits-for-all structure resonates and provides the desired outcome, it is important to recognize there is no single insurance solution that can provide every employee in your population with the peace of mind they may personally require.

People need different things in order to feel protected. As part of the Benefits Exercise you again need to consider the diversity of your workforce: nationality of the employees, local statutory requirements, financial concerns, existing health and wellness issues, the myriad of perspectives from management to the cleaner, and the overarching HR and Benefits Philosophy. At this stage of the process, you begin to appreciate that every perspective will have a different view of the programme's benefits and you must focus attention on gaining positive impact for the majority.

Stephanie Nash, Chief People Officer at Redmart, comments, "Two of the biggest value adds in having an intermediary guide you through the process of structuring a benefits programme are analysing the perspectives from every angle and the trusted advice and partnership." If you are an HR leader or responsible for benefits and compensation, ask yourself and your team:

- What do we think about the benefits?
- How will our CEO respond to the structure?
- How will Gen X-er and Gen Y-er employees view the programme?
- Have we considered the financial impact for now and for future?

If you're structuring a global or regional programme, you also need to consider how each of the local HR leaders or local managers will respond to the benefits structure.

While the majority of the Benefits Exercise is an internal and technical look at programme design line by line, the culmination of this part of the process is identifying appropriate insurance companies to work with in the market, negotiating and securing proposals. If you have a procurement team, they will typically handle this process for you. If you outsource this part of the process, whether it's through procurement or an intermediary, it is critical to work in partnership with the team that is going to assist you. They must understand the aims, goals and guidance they are working under.

Placement teams that do not engage closely with HR leaders and management teams at every level can have a detrimental impact on employee benefit programmes, especially at a local or regional level if they are making global appointments.

This can hinder the company's ability to make informed decisions which are aligned to your HR and Benefits Philosophy. In this new age where people practices are changing and challenged by stale strategies, internal partnership between procurement and benefit decision-makers is critical to ensuring successful and sustainable programme structures.

When programme structure and design are not integrated with your people strategy, the negative impact on corporate culture, lack of buy-in from management teams or HR leaders and inability to engage your employee population will all cause challenges that are difficult to overcome. A paralyzed leadership team will lead to increased turnover and be detrimental on employee morale. Whether it is a procurement team working on negotiation and placement, HR, finance, an office manager or the CEO, if there is a shortage of insurance expertise in-house, engaging an intermediary or service provider with the technical knowledge you need can provide you invaluable insight and partnership at this stage.

In my interview with Stephanie Nash, she commented, "A broker is critical, they are an additional resource which helps you negotiate, place and administer the programme. This is not typically within the core competency of an HR team and even if it costs more, this role is best outsourced." While leaders in your business best understand your people, your culture, your Benefits Philosophy and your business strategy, an intermediary can become an additional and critical resource. It is in this step of the blueprint where you are deciding on the right insurance partner for the programme. A major benefit to you is that typically engaging an intermediary comes with no extra cost. Increasingly, "employers continue to partner with their vendors to link payment to value." (2015 Emerging Trends in Health Care, Towers Watson)

For companies with resources for placement and procurement in-house, I would highly recommend some additional reading which provides a powerful next-generation approach to negotiation, "The Art of Negotiation" by Michael Wheeler. In his book, Michael quotes Ambassador Richard Holbrooke, "Negotiation is like jazz. It is improvisation on a theme. You know where you want to go, but you don't know how to get there. It's not linear." Choosing the right partner to help you navigate how to get there is just as important as getting where you want to go.

When a company chooses self-insurance to support their programme design, it is important to review the history and reasons for doing so. By conducting a loss ratio review (more on this in Step 5 of the blueprint) and a benefit-cost analysis on the self-insurance structure, it may become easy to identify whether these benefits should be consolidated into a larger insurance protection programme. It may also clearly indicate which coverage is best to continue to operate and be administered independently from a protection policy. This should be done at the individual benefit level and does not necessarily mean all benefits move from self-insurance to protection or vice versa. If self-insurance is recommended, there should be enough guidance to understand the financial, administration, re-source and morale exposures.

Often companies overlook the administration require-ments in supporting their programme. Policy administra-tion can cause unforeseen challenges which translate into negative morale even if a benefits structure has been beau-tifully designed. If the initial focus is to alleviate the burden of internal company resources required to administer the programmes or processes, including simplified enrolment processes or an efficient programme structure, it will pay dividends. In addition, let's not forget that claim processes can make or break employee morale instantly. I implore you to deep dive into claims administration in order to make the practical aspects of the programme palatable sooner rath-er than later. Do not let claims cause a crisis.

Understanding underwriting implications allows you to make appropriate decisions when it comes to how you want a policy to respond to member's pre-existing medical conditions. In addition, premium will be impacted by your decision on how you want the programme to respond to pre-existing conditions. The same programme structure may have different price points for different underwrit-ing options.

Health is a very intimate subject for most people. Put-ting a member in a position where they have to disclose or discuss their medical history with their employer is a challenging morale matter. A client said it best when they shared their biggest pain point with me: "We are forced to discuss his medical condition in the morning and his career development that afternoon."

> In addition, underwriting will certainly impact the ability for a member to claim, so education of your employees must feature high on the agenda when administering a programme which does have limitations or no coverage for prior health conditions.

As a benefits decision-maker for your company, you are in control of how a programme underwrites members. There are a variety of different methodologies, some of which are described in detail in Section 3 of this book. The availability of a certain underwriting method will depend on the insurance companies you are approaching to provide the benefits. It is important to consider underwriting as a major factor when structuring a benefits programme and choosing an insurance partner.

The Benefits Exercise, when conducted thoroughly, is the best way of achieving clarity for both employers and employees. Once the final programme proposals are available, it is decision making time. You want to be in a position where you can review all the proposals together, side by side. You need to understand the dynamics of each insurer's service delivery and practical aspects of the programmes from benefits to underwriting to claims. Benefit limits are only one piece of the puzzle and as a company you need to understand the metrics of the programme design from underwriting to the impact of utilization, enrolment to renewal invitation, claims to customer service.

Making sure you have a strong team with the technical knowledge to conduct the exercise will ensure that if and when any surprises do arise, responses have already been anticipated and are aligned and delivered in accordance with your HR and Benefits Philosophy. You should not underestimate the value in conducting a Benefits Exercise when it comes to generating positive impact and transparency within your corporate culture. Regardless of the size of your company, everyone prospers from a simple, clearly explained benefit structure which is guided by purpose.

# Chapter 7

## THE BENEFITS EXERCISE: SINK OR SWIM?

The oil and gas industry provides us with interesting clients, this one was on the consulting side of the offshore industry. They provide manpower solutions for pipeline projects. The company had purchased an oil and gas specialty product from an insurance company directly. They made a specific point to purchase the evacuation and repatriation coverage that came along with their industry-specialized health insurance product. Of course, one of the unique needs for many clients in the oil and gas industry is the requirement for relocation from "ship to shore." If one of their team is on an offshore platform supervising the installation of pipeline and they have an accident, injury or illness they will require the support for transport by medevac, usually helicopter or boat, from the platform to shore to access medical care,. Typically, companies either purchase coverage for the evacuation or rely on self-insurance to cover the costs for the transport from ship to shore.

When I engaged with Romain, a Business Development Manager and the firm's HR liaison for South East Asia, he shared a story about the challenge they experienced without knowing the right questions to ask to truly understand how their coverage was designed and would respond when needed. One of their deep sea divers, Pierre, had an accident just after he surfaced. Pierre had slipped onboard the vessel and after being looked over by the nurse practitioner, it was believed he had broken his tailbone. Pierre had to be taken to shore for immediate treatment. A call was made to engage the insurer taking care of their evacuation coverage and the crew manager was told that the benefits would only respond and pay for the evacuation once Pierre had reached the shore. The insurance company advised they were able to assist but the transit from ship to shore would come at the client's own cost. Coverage would only begin once Pierre was onshore.

Romain was unaware that transport from ship to shore was outside the scope of the policy. The company, and Romain, had assumed that the nature of the product as advertised for the oil and gas industry would include the ship to shore cover as part of the evacuation and repatriation benefit.

Romain had relied on the false assumptions that an insurance provider would have an intimate understanding of their industry and knowledge of the offshore requirements and therefore trusted everything was taken care of.

Medevacs are not cheap; this one cost about $75,000.

In the end, the company engaged me to cover their gap as they were unable to support self-insurance after such a financial hiccup as this. We ended up going to a specialty insurance company which cost them more that year. They were trying to tap into in a specialized industry product, and take advantage of an insurer's apparent understanding of their firm's requirements in the offshore business. In addition, the niche product was substantially less costly than the other insurer's options they came across when they initially secured the cover, only for it to end up costing them far more later on.

The damage that can be done by purchasing specialized products and policies like this, or linking into scheme deals, in an effort to avoid understanding the technicality of the terms of coverage can be disastrous. At the same time, insurers whom are offering these products specific to industry have a responsibility to ensure direct buyers know what they are and are not covered for under the plan design. In this case, the insurer did not own their responsibility to explain to Romain and his company the areas of coverage which would not respond when they elected to purchase the evacuation benefits. Romain was left to believe that the product was developed because of the insurer's understanding of the offshore industry and that the insurer could accommodate all of the unique coverage needs of his industry. Beware of the false impression of advertising, "we understand your industry so well that we've created this special product that's unique to the needs of your industry."

| Ask the right questions about the coverage.

In the oil and gas industry, employers are counting on the fact that the employee will leave the vessel and be able to access the medical care and treatment they need or could not get while working offshore. Companies are relying on benefits to provide for the costs associated with keeping their employees fit and healthy when on their off-time so that when it's time for them to return for their six weeks offshore they're ready to work. Any down time, especially in these incredibly unique industries, costs money. Most companies do not have the expertise in-house to be able to understand the questions they need to ask of these specialty programmes designed for their industry. Then they don't understand their risks and exposures. That's not to say that these specialty programmes are bad but they require the same level of review as a non-industry specific product offering. Education is paramount and you need to understand what they've left out for your specific industry.

If Romain had engaged us earlier, as an intermediary we would have acted as a guide for the company through the procurement process and asked the right questions which could have helped them avoid splashing out on the surprising expense of the medevac, as well as the extra expense of another policy that year. Conducting the Benefits Exercise in this case would have saved $80,000 plus the hassle of a top-up and the unexpected hurdle at time of need.

# Chapter 8

## STEP 3:
## BUILDING THE INFRASTRUCTURE

Before the financial crisis of 2008, there were many more benefit and compensation resources dedicated to employee support and available to the workforce on the frontline to field questions from people. A risk manager, an insurance team within HR or a dedicated benefits and compensation team in-house would answer questions like these:

- Am I covered for this?
- How do I make a claim?
- Is this coverage enough for me and my family?

The specialized resources supported the entire benefits process, including communication initiatives about the programme in place. The dedicated resources were available both in the initial onboarding of a new employee and throughout the employee's tenure with the company.

Following the financial crisis, there has been a substantial cost-cutting exercise across companies of all sizes which has led to limited resources in HR, risk management and benefits. There are fewer people dedicated to interacting with employees from a human resources perspective. Since many of the resources to support employee benefit programmes have been cut in an effort to crunch expense lines in tougher financial times, this leaves business leaders and managers on the frontline. This has created challenges for employers in this new and changing landscape.

Without the substantial benefit and compensation teams of the past, there is an increasing reliance on HR as well as managers within the business itself to answer to employees about their benefits. Not having specialized people who understand benefit programmes and insurance structures intimately causes a challenge to employer's engagement activities within the scope of human resources, benefits administration is just one aspect among a long list of other critical functions. HR responsibilities can include recruitment, contracts, handling employee and people matters, misconduct, performance issues, learning and development, and the list goes on. Benefits is just one more vertical that falls within the HR world. There are plenty of HR people and managers who have never, ever had any focus on benefits or compensation.

In the case of companies whom do not have dedicated HR support, line managers take over this responsibility. For obvious reasons, this is not their area of expertise. These managers may have never been responsible for interacting with benefit programmes before and therefore may not understand the way in which administering or explaining benefits can impact morale with immediate repercussions on employees and the company alike. In addition, they are typically unqualified or lack the technical expertise to provide guidance on coverage or claims. There is a fine line that companies with business managers on the benefits frontline have to walk when it comes to supporting their people on understanding the coverage in their benefits programme.

## Building A Benefits Team

The purpose of building an infrastructure to support a benefits programme is to create a seamless experience for everyone within your organization: HR, the administration and finance team, your management teams and your employees. The best way in which to build your infrastructure is to first create or appoint a dedicated Benefits Team. Whether you create an in-house team or outsource to an intermediary or provider, it is important to build a Benefits Team that can interact and engage on your behalf as a company with your employees and the insurance company with whom you have chosen to partner. Once your Benefits Team is appointed, they become the trusted and reliable resource for the company and also for all of the employees. It is important for the Benefits Team to speak the language of the company and have a thorough understanding of the HR and Benefits Philosophy. The voice echoed by this team should become the voice of the company when it comes to benefits.

The responsibilities allocated to the benefits team should remove the burden of paperwork, administration, claim escalations and support services from internal business resources where possible. In doing so, you reduce the cost and in-house requirements wherever possible. "Added value services are not necessarily viewed as adding enough value as only just over 25% of employers say they give them serious consideration as part of the provider selection process." (Employee Benefits and Trends Survey, Aon)

> When you are in the selection process to build your Benefits Team, you need to consider what every partner in the value chain may be offering and bringing to the table.

In day to day business, I see so many companies paying intermediaries or third party administrators a service fee which is charged for every headcount within their firm. When I question a client about the type of services they are receiving for this fee, the most common answers include claims administration and responding to benefit queries from their members. Paying a fee for this service astounds me as these are services that most intermediaries, providers and insurance companies offer as part of their own service proposition and should not necessarily require additional financial contribution.

Statistics support my day to day business findings. "Insurer services are potentially under-utilised by employers, with 35% of employers surveyed not using the claims management services offered by their insurers if an employee is absent through ill health, an increase from 29% in 2014." (Employee Benefits and Trends Survey, Aon)

Supporting services should be tailored to your company's needs. These services may include the development of technology, apps or microsites to provide real-time access to information and documents related to the benefits programme in an online platform. A benefit hotline or dedicated email address can be made available to employees for questions they may have throughout the year. The availability of resources among the Benefits Team — which includes not only internal HR leaders but also other supporting members — offers intimacy when it comes to specific personal concerns or treatment covered under the programme. Mental health is a good example of coverage which employees may want to access but they may be uncomfortable asking about this benefit with an internal company resource or colleague.

One area in which the Benefit Team can provide additional value is reviewing internal processes, procedures and protocols. For example, the development of employee handbook supplements giving an overview of the benefits, or advice and assistance with the treatment of benefits provided within employment contracts. Onboarding documents should also be reviewed to include benefit-related material with contact points, benefit summaries, claim processes and references on the programme itself.

Many companies operate work injury or accident reporting procedures to meet statutory requirements. If you expand the reach of these procedures to fall in line with the benefit programmes, there may be additional value in maximizing the coverage across protection policies to respond in specific situations and therefore assist in mitigating claims on a particular policy. The more integrated the team become with understanding your internal organization, the more value the Benefits Team adds.

Health services, wellness or preventative services may also be organized by the Benefits Team and become an extension of the larger employee benefits offering. Discounts or referrals made available to employees for gyms, annual routine health screenings, personal trainers, counsellors or chiropractors support a strong culture of wellbeing within a firm. Infrastructure needs to go beyond just the insurance administration and encompass your broader health and wellness strategy in order to provide seamless connection to your broader HR and engagement initiatives. Infrastructure also has to be designed to alleviate the direct connection between HR as benefits administrator and claims counsel. This will allow your HR leaders to focus on the strategic business needs of your people and not on pushing paperwork related to the programme.

Comprehensive understanding and development of the claim processes, including the flow of claims, contact points and escalation procedures, should be developed to ensure claims process as smoothly as possible from the beginning. By defining timelines for the claim process and making employees aware of the average turnaround times, you will avoid unnecessary escalations in advance.

Employers do seem to recognize the value of their partners in the benefit value chain when it comes to case management. "Employer interest in insurers getting involved in the management of short-term absence cases remains strong (78%)." (Employee Benefits and Trends Survey, Aon) Companies do recognize the need to have assistance when something happens. In order to mitigate claims, it is important an employee receives guidance as they begin their treatment. But employers need to begin utilizing the assistance and resources available to relieve the administrative burden and support employee communication efforts as well. Typically these services come at no additional cost.

The Benefits Team will be driving all of the education and engagement initiatives discussed in the next step of the process. Building a benefits team provides you with an opportunity to outsource and gain the expertise that is not available, and often not required, in-house in your day-to-day business operations. It saves you salaried roles, it saves you resources, time, energy and money. And it saves you answering all of the many questions that come as people engage with their employee benefit programme. It helps you manage morale and provides consistency and transparency in the administration of the programme and the benefits.

Here is an overview of what else a benefit team can and should deliver:

- Morale management: key personnel identified, morale movers given personal attention

- Health and wellness services support: **as part of prevention which also leads to cost-containment**

- Build and develop ongoing support services: **microsites, dedicated hotlines, claim processes**

- Transition support: **required when there are changes to the programme or providers**

Your employee benefit infrastructure should encompass strategy and extend far beyond just insurance administration. Service should not stop once a programme is placed, the Benefits Team is available to complement HR and business leaders to ensure employees understand the benefits and how to use the programme throughout the duration of the policy year.

Your infrastructure should be seamlessly integrated to your organization and your benefits team as an extension of your own team to operate on the frontline with employees and their families.

# Chapter 9

## STEP 4:
## ENGAGE, EDUCATE & EMPOWER

"This year, culture and engagement was rated the most important issue overall, slightly edging out leadership (the No. 1 issue last year). This challenge highlights the need for business and HR leaders to gain a clear understanding of their organization's culture and reexamine every HR and talent programme as a way to better engage and empower people." (Deloitte's 2015 Global Human Capital Trends)

The fourth step in the Benefits Blueprint is all about communication through education and employee engagement. While the focus in the early stages of the process is to build the foundation, allow time for research and reviews of the programme and then create the infrastructure to support the programme, we now need to focus our attention on communication with your employee population.

"The communication and administration of benefits are effectively the "shop window" of a benefits plan. This is the public view that employees see, and therefore will shape their perception of it. If a benefits plan is well thought-out and caters to diverse employee needs, but is not communicated, the value of the plan is at risk. It's important to remember that there is no "right" way to communicate — how an organization can most effectively communicate will depend wholly on its circumstances, including the makeup of its employee population, its strategic goals, its organizational culture, and so on." (2015 Asia Pacific Trends, Towers Watson)

The Towers Watson report for 2015 Asia Pacific Trends goes on to highlight, "More than a quarter (27%) of employers still do not communicate with their workforce about benefits."

> Communicating about benefits is crucial and can dramatically increase the impact of your benefit spend within your employee population with little to no cost.

Remember, people are your most valuable asset and it is important they view benefits as part of the total rewards strategy. We are looking to continuously generate positive impact through engagement and connection to the employee value proposition. The goal of this stage of the process is to communicate within appropriate timelines for people to feel settled and comfortable with the protection you're providing. This includes allowing for time and offering a forum for questions and concerns to be voiced and answered.

If you are launching a new programme or implementing major changes to an existing programme, you need to determine the ideal timeline for the change communications. I typically recommend you send a simple written communication about the fact there is a programme or changes to a programme coming with effect from "x" date. This should ideally be distributed four to six weeks prior to launch. This simple message allows people time to process that change is coming. We all know people respond to change in different ways and they take time to come around, even if there is a positive message to be delivered with the change. Sending the message earlier than this, you risk losing the interest of your audience as the changes do not register as imminent enough for many people to take notice. Leaving communication any later than this and it may be too close to the start date, causing minds to wander about whether it was a rushed or uncoordinated decision. It may also generate scepticism about the changes, eliciting questions which otherwise may not arise. You want communication to be strategic and clear. Timing is everything in the lead-up to launch date.

Coordinated communication during any benefits launch should allow trust to continue to build between employer and employee as well as any supporting providers and partners, including your Benefits Team. It is important to keep the communications short but informative enough to allow employees to gain the understanding they need about the benefits which will lead to a general feeling of wellbeing.

Keep messages simple. Complexity can lead to confusion and remember we are aiming for education and peace of mind through understanding and transparency.

Producing a communication document is essential here. I usually call this "A Guide to Employee Benefits." This document reinforces the company's role as provisioner of benefits, and should include a summary of benefits which provides a high level overview of all the areas of coverage in the programme. As important as it is to highlight the benefits provided, it must also highlight the benefits not offered under the programme. The document should include a table of benefits and also a user guide for the most frequently used claim processes. Communicating the ease of use features within a programme is critical for engaging your people about the practical how-to of the programme itself. Understanding how to access the benefits provided is often just as valuable as the benefits themselves.

The infrastructure you created in Step 3 must come across as accessible in order to offer true and realized value. "If a benefits plan is cumbersome to administer and involves many different platforms and lots of paperwork, it will not only be viewed negatively by employees, but will also be a burden to the HR department, and take focus away from more strategic matters. It's important to ensure that the administration, processes and technology are fully aligned with the organization's benefits strategy and objectives." (2015 Asia Pacific Benefit Trends, Towers Watson)

If an employee does not feel comfortable because they do not understand how to get assistance when treatment is required, you fail to establish the true advantage to benefits: peace of mind and security in the protection you are providing. A list of points of contact, including your Benefits Team, should be summarized so that at the outset people have every avenue of support which they may require throughout the year.

This guide is a resource which will help you avoid disappointment later. We encourage every employer to take the opportunity to share this communication and introduce your Benefits Team in person, where possible, through an interactive session with your employees. Call it a communication session. This provides true engagement and amplifies the positive morale results which can be achieved in a benefits launch. Making your "Guide to Employee Benefits" document or presentation accessible in a location or directory familiar to everyone in your organization will encourage them to refer to this resource whenever they may need it throughout the course of the year. It will also alleviate a lot of the basic questions that managers, HR or your Benefits Team have to field. Your infrastructure, which you designed in the earlier stage of this process, should be easily identifiable and accessible to your employees. It should never be an 88- page download.

A lack of understanding can lead to discontent and this is not ideal for creating continuity in how employee benefits support and enhance the employee value proposition. As reported in Deloitte's Asia Trends 2015 report, "Today's challenges require a new playbook—one that makes HR more agile, forward thinking, and bolder in its solutions."

> Education will build a foundation of transparency and understanding in your employee population.

## Communication Doesn't Cost a Penny But Saves a Fortune

Just how important is it that you engage your employees and offer transparency when explaining the benefits? Let's say your benefits programme has a cap for chronic conditions in the amount of $5,000. Edward joins the company and after five months he is diagnosed with diabetes. The total costs for the lab tests, diagnostics and consultations run to just under $8,000 for establishing his initial diagnosis.

Initially when he joined the company all that was provided to him to explain his benefits was a technical insurer's policy schedule as an appendix in the Employee Handbook published on your HR portal. In this example it is easy for you to imagine Edward approaching HR with a $3,000 bill and wanting to discuss why his employee benefits programme has only reimbursed $5,000. To make matters worse, he then discloses to his line manager that there will be ongoing monthly bills of $1,000 to ensure his condition is stabilized and well-monitored. He wants clarity on how these follow-up costs will be covered. Morale management becomes incredibly difficult in such a scenario as the outcome is almost certainly going to lead to disappointment. Even relying on "HR guardrails" which are aligned with your Benefits Philosophy in a moment such as this do not support your efforts if you have not built a foundation of understanding through communication and education first.

Imagine instead we consider this same scenario within a company whom has a holistic approach to engaging employees. You provide "A Guide to Employee Benefits" document to Edward via email during his first week with the company, as part of the onboarding process. As well, you host bi-annual presentations as part of a health and wellness day for all of your people, which provides and encourages a forum for questions or concerns to be raised. Clear explanation and creating a culture of education and transparency highlighting the limitations of the employer-sponsored benefits programme leads Edward to consider his own personal needs for strong critical and chronic illness coverage due to financial vulnerabilities, which the company may have no view on. He takes matters into his own hands to arrange a top-up insurance policy privately. When Edward receives his diabetes diagnosis, the first $5,000 is paid by the employee benefits programme and the next $3,000 is reimbursed by his private policy. He is not out of pocket for any of his treatment and the top-up policy will continue to respond and settle all of his ongoing treatment and maintenance bills. You see how disappointment and financial vulnerability were avoided entirely by the open communication policy the company has in place. That did not cost the company a penny but saved them a fortune.

You need to approach education and communication with the same view you had while building an HR and Benefits Philosophy, a view that appreciates the many differing perspectives of your people. To be comprehensive in your efforts, you need to provide not only communication about the programme itself but also provide employees with context.

With a diverse and mobile workforce, you need to consider how you educate your expatriate team about local healthcare systems and costs associated with treatment when they begin living and working in a new country to help your business grow. For many people whom have lived in a country which provides a robust national healthcare system, when they move abroad they may be blind to the costs associated with medical treatment. Take for example a Brit, a Kiwi, a Canadian or a Swede, they would all typically have no concept of costs related to medical treatment because the government structure in their home country responds and more often than not, they don't see any of the their bills. Move an employee such as this to Hong Kong and share with them the fact that one of the most routine surgeries on the planet, such as having your tonsils removed, may cost them upwards of $20,000 and you will leave them speechless and scared unless you also share with them how and to what extent the employee benefits programme will protect them from these costs.

When you communicate not only the details of the employee-sponsored benefits programme but also the context for costs of care in the country, you build a foundation of trust. This foundation and education allows employees to understand the potential financial exposures and take charge of their own personal protection needs if the employee benefits programme does not provide them with adequate coverage.

> When you use education as a tool to put your employees in the driver's seat, you are sure to avoid major morale trouble caused by disappointments in the benefits you provide.

## Morale Movers

Speaking of morale management, effective morale management must go beyond good communication. This can be done by identifying key personnel within an organization, what I call "morale movers". By this I mean those individuals whom tend to be very vocal with colleagues and their management on just about anything. Their influence can lend to positivity or negativity for their colleagues depending on their message of the moment. We all recognize that most companies have these morale movers within the employee population. I suggest you provide these morale movers personal attention during the benefits launch process. Make your Benefits Team aware of who they are in advance. If your "morale movers" are given additional support during any periods of transition, you can empower them to be a positive promoter of the programme at the outset. I would not recommend alerting them to this part of the process but certainly recognizing an individual's ability to motivate positive opinions and views can be used to create acceptance and a general feeling of calm in an organization. You know who they are already, I'm sure.

Whenever you are transitioning from one benefits programme to another or making major changes that may impact people, transition support is crucial. Your Benefits Team needs to be fully engaged for any transitional periods for this support. I always recommend providing a comparison of the incumbent benefits and the new benefits side by side. If you have followed this blueprint to establish your HR and Benefits Philosophy and then aligned programme benefits accordingly, whatever the reasons for the change, you can be assured communication initiatives will support the continuous message to your people power. Whether you are communicating upgrades, downgrades or similar benefits between two programmes, the transparency of the comparison breeds trust. Your Benefits Team is then available to answer questions and discuss the changes at any point during a transition period, and beyond.

A great education offers a great foundation for employees to understand what has been offered, in what capacity, with what limits and under what context so that employees can act in their own interests if there is a need. Empowerment through communication and education makes your employee benefits bulletproof.

# Chapter 10

# ENGAGE, EDUCATE & EMPOWER: NO QUESTIONS ASKED

Think of your employee benefits communication strategy like an internal marketing campaign. You need to envision all the skeptics and answer to them in advance, you need to cover all the angles and be creative. A successful communication strategy engages, educates and empowers employees which contributes to a culture of trust in an organization. It does not deliver disappointments like this story does.

I was speaking at the Expat Cancer Support Group and one of the women, Ashley, shared her story with me. She and her husband, Phil, had been relocated to Singapore twenty years ago when he received an offer to make the move on a full expatriate package, all expenses taken care of. They are the quintessential example of a family whom never had a need to think about health insurance protection because it was always provided by the company. Over the years they had two children and never had more than a few optical bills to pay out of their own pocket.

The financial crisis brought change for them, like the majority of the expatriate community living in Asia. Phil was localized. After twenty years of reliance on the company, there was no dramatic shift in their mindset when their employee benefits changed. Phil's boss had commented, "You will still have health benefits for the family," and they asked no questions.

It was not long after they were localized that they received bad news. Ashley was diagnosed with breast cancer. She shared that on the very same morning that she found the lump, she was ushered through a host of lab tests, ultrasounds and investigations to confirm the diagnosis. Before the day had finished, an oncologist had operated and was discussing the ongoing chemotherapy treatment which she would require.

After a whirlwind day with more than eight hours in the hospital, she was presented with the bill, $80,000. Phil began with a few phone calls to the insurance company but he was advised that because the treatment had not been pre-authorized in advance, they would need to settle the bills and apply for the reimbursements afterward. With no insurance to respond, they handed a collection of credit cards over the counter.

When the reimbursement had processed, it was accompanied by a complex explanation of benefits referring to policy wording and exclusion clauses, indicating a lot of costs that were unpaid. In fact, the reimbursement settlement recovered only $28,000. Ashley shared with me their initial shock but also shared that they were reasonably confident they had not understood the letter that accompanied the check. Phil requested an opportunity to speak with HR to explain the technical language in the letter.

HR referred him back to the insurer initially to get an explanation on how the coverage was paying out and under what benefits. The claims representative highlighted that there was a $25,000 cancer care limit in place on the policy. As the initial consultations and investigations were prior to the official cancer diagnosis, the claims administrator had reimbursed an additional $3,000 out of the programme's outpatient benefits. The policy had already reimbursed for all eligible treatment expenses and maximum refund was confirmed at $28,000. That left $52,000 out of pocket for the family.

When Phil pressed his boss for an understanding on how his wife's diagnosis would have been covered under the previous benefits programme before they had been localized, his boss was reluctant to respond. A meeting with HR was the next step and all parties sat down together to review. The HR Director had voiced a reasonable perspective and pressed for a response on why Phil had not asked any questions about their new benefits when his contract had changed. As Phil explained, "We've been here for twenty years and everything has always been taken care of, in my mind the only things that were changing were my rent and repatriation. I never expected to suddenly end up with $52,000 in medical bills because my package changed." He pushed back, asking why no one took the time to explain the new benefits to him.

There is dual responsibility here and both employee and employer must own their part.

> It is the responsibility of an employer to provide enough information to educate and engage so people are able to consider the impact. It is the responsibility of the employee to demand enough information to understand the protection being provided.

It's a partnership and you need to always remember to hold up your side of the bargain, otherwise the value of the benefit remains unrealized.

In this situation, the local employee benefit programme was designed to cover a basic level of medical treatment and care required to complement the national healthcare system and subsidized insurance schemes available to local nationals. As foreigners, Phil and Ashley were not eligible to receive subsidized care or private policies, but they were covered under the local programme the same as those whom are eligible. While an employee benefits programme is typically designed to meet the needs of the majority, it might not be suitable for everyone's needs in the company.

It does not cost an employer any money to make a mention of this fact, and obviously it can have positive morale impact when a company is the one encouraging their employees to understand the benefits and get advice privately, if you need it, on what you should do if you recognize there are gaps or a cap on protection.

Communication is critical to the success of a programme. "The number of employers that said that their benefits were highly valued increased four-fold for companies that believe they communicate benefits effectively compared to those that do not." (2015 Asia Pacific Benefit Trends, Towers Watson)

Bold and engaging communication strategies also offer the opportunity to highlight that you may not be providing a full coverage, all-inclusive benefits programme that will take care of every possible medical expense you may encounter. Companies can clearly recognize the business value of a healthy workforce and should be encouraging employees to take control of their health. Education is key to empowerment within your employee population. Among "two of the top five areas employers say will be the focus of their health care activities in 2016 link to employee engagement and accountability: developing or enhancing a workplace culture where employees are responsible for their health." (2015 Emerging Trends in Health Care Survey, Towers Watson)

Remember, there is no one-size-fits-all insurance solution because every one of your team may have a different perspective on the level of protection that provides them with peace of mind. The responsibility really lies within each of us as individuals to know what we are covered for, but if you are an engaged employer and are providing proactive communication to educate your people, you will avoid disastrous disappointments such as this one. In this brave new employment world you must view your benefit communication initiatives as a way to educate, engage and empower employees which will only enhance your employee value proposition.

# Chapter 11

## STEP 5:
## REVIEW & REPEAT AS REQUIRED

This final step is where you get to have your cake and eat it too, at least most years. Even though I call this step R & R, and even if you have successfully structured a sustainable programme, we cannot go so far as calling this step rest and relaxation. When I say R & R, I mean review and repeat at renewal as required.

Thirty to sixty days prior to renewal is the time for you to review your employee benefits programme and consider what is working and what is not. If you have kept your list of employee feedback throughout the year, it will be easy to discuss and determine whether there are any employee feedback-driven changes to consider for the year ahead. This is always the best place to begin the renewal review. It opens the forum among HR and business leaders within the company, engaging them directly in the benefits discussion.

It is a good opportunity to re-energize the Benefits Team and remind everyone why the benefits structure was implemented. Reviewing the intention of benefits and limits offers an opportunity to realign programme structure. In addition, it is an opportunity to determine whether there have been any major shifts during the course of the year in the HR and Benefits Philosophy or employee value proposition that would impact the benefits programme and demands.

## Complete A Loss Ratio Review

Because you have an active and engaging benefits programme in place, it is important to complete a loss ratio review during the renewal process. For many clients with whom I have worked, the benefit decision-makers, there is a gap in understanding how powerful a loss ratio review can be for providing data driven insights into a programme's performance. Many clients do not even realize they can request a history of claims or utilization rates of their programmes. Metrics can be relied upon to deliver results when you need to reconsider how to manage premium increases at renewal.

If there has been no analysis conducted to track or monitor member usage under the programme, you have no idea what benefits people use or view as valuable. In addition, you would have no idea what elements of coverage they did not use and therefore may be worthwhile reconsidering. While premiums may inherently have to increase every year to keep pace with medical inflation, you should be in control over the increases if you understand your utilization patterns and trends. This will provide you with guidance on how to implement cost-containment measures, if necessary. We never want you to be in a position where you just pay up.

### Identifying The Key Cost Drivers

A review should include identifying the key cost drivers of a programme. You need to take a detailed look at:

- Benefit and provider utilization rates
- Frequency and severity of claims
- Trends and patterns for claims
- Common conditions claimed
- Features or policy mechanics which may drive increased cost.

Following the review, a list of cost containment considerations and recommendations should be developed, which may also include wellness initiatives outside the scope of the insurance benefits programme. For profitable programmes, there may be no action required but should the programme begin to perform poorly you can immediately refer to these cost containment considerations to determine the most appropriate course of action without being in a position where the only choice is to accept a premium increase at renewal.

The loss ratio review provides you context to identify and prioritize premium impact points, keeping in mind your member population. A benefits programme can then be efficiently tailored to adjust as and when required to maximize benefits spend while minimizing the impact any changes may have on the employee population. Prioritizing and understanding preferences for areas which may require benefit changes to positively impact pricing places you in a strong position to be able to build the communication message to employees when changes are unavoidable.

You need to review the renewal offer from the provider which typically also details the claim performance of the programme over the last nine months. When claims data is unfavourable, you need to understand the poor performance in detail to determine how to modify in order to ensure a high performance programme for the coming year. If you have had a policy with the same provider for many years, there are often profitably reviews you can reference from prior years which may mitigate an unexpected or uninvited premium increase and offer you a strong position for negotiations. If you do need to consider implementing cost-containment measures, it's important to start with step one and use your HR and Benefits Philosophy as well as the benefits exercise to ensure programme modifications are consistent and not competing with your employee value proposition. Morale management when changes are required should be a major priority during Steps 3 and 4 when relaunching the programme.

### Remarketing A Programme

Remarketing a programme with other providers should also be considered, if appropriate. Complacency can be checked and premium increases may be mitigated by engaging competition for the programme with other providers. Many times you may receive pressures from elsewhere in your organization if there is scepticism or doubt about whether similar benefits can be obtained for less. It can also strengthen your position when negotiating. Remarketing helps to ensure competitive benefits, terms and conditions, underwriting and premium rates.

## A Turn of Events

The ebb and flow of business and markets causes changes which cannot be anticipated. Internal changes at the company's senior management or board level may mean a major deviation in business strategy. There are always plenty of external changes at play which impact business. Oil prices drop and your business experiences financial constraints. Talent attraction or retention challenges are caused by competition. An insurance company is acquired or changes their product offering. Any of these external events or a combination of events may cause you to begin the benefit building process again.

If you start back at Step 1, this blueprint will guide you through the entire renewal review successfully. While future-proofing your health care strategy is not entirely possible, you can exceed average performance by making programme changes that meet business needs and fit with your company's total rewards strategy.

In this dynamic new landscape, it is important for local and multinational employers with a globally mobile workforce to be flexible and strategic about their benefits spend. Keeping employee benefit programmes aligned with your organization - your people, your leadership, your goals and your competition - requires you to stay committed to the Benefits Blueprint. From establishing your HR and Benefits Philosophy, structuring the programme during the benefits exercise, creating the infrastructure, empowering employees and reviewing the programme annually you will ensure a sustainable and successful programme that powers your business forward.

# Section 3

## TOOLS OF THE TRADE

# Chapter 12

## MY MANIFESTO ON FLEX

The following chapters explain different tools of the industry that are worth consideration as you do your benefits exercise. From benchmarking through profiling, these chapters will round out your knowledge of different strategies used when it comes to securing optimal coverage. Let's start with flexible benefits.

Flex is a buzz word that has taken the employee benefits space by storm. Also known as 'flexible benefits', 'cafeteria benefits' or 'flex plans'. When you consider the new generation employee and how the employment relationship can best be developed and sustained, flexible benefit structures have a lot of potential. You should keep flex in mind as you conduct your benefits exercise. Once you know the ins and outs of flexible benefits, you can make a more educated decision as to whether or not this structure is a good fit for your company.

While the focus for choosing a flexible benefits programme, or any other benefit structure, should be to better respond and answer the diverse needs of your population, the Employee Benefits and Trends Survey 2015 conducted by Aon cites a totally different driver for electing this structure. "To 'meet market norms' was the answer most given by respondents – 30% cited this as their main motivation. The desires to 'drive productivity and engagement' and 'retain talent' were joint second answers, both given by 23% of respondents. **10% offered benefits to create alignment with the organization's objectives** with 11% citing attracting talent as a driver, while just 1% cited controlling costs as their primary reason." (Employee Benefits and Trends Survey 2015, Aon) While flexible benefits has huge potential to help us align with the changed and changing relationship between employers and employees, these polled statistics prove we are still far from choosing flex for the right reasons at the outset.

The focus of flexible benefits as compared to a traditional benefits package is simple – it gives employees more choice. How flexible is flex? You need to determine how much choice you want to offer and around which types and levels of benefits you offer it. Flexible plans force you to engage in an internal conversation about your obligation and responsibility as an employer. Is it your role to provide the promise of protection in this new landscape?

As an employer, you may want to restrict employee benefit choice to some degree because you feel you have a vested interest in making sure there is a minimal level of economic security for your people. This will help ensure you are not placed in an increasing number of situations where you are exercising your "HR guardrails". Establishing a baseline of coverage may also help you to avoid challenging morale situations. For instance, you might be embarrassed or garner unwanted public attention if the employee did not elect health insurance coverage and was subsequently unable to pay a large hospital bill. For most flexible benefit plans, you will specify a minimum level of certain benefits deemed essential for all. The majority of schemes are built on the foundation of company-paid benefits, where the employer provides a minimum or compulsory level of core benefits for which employees cannot elect to opt out.

If you do choose flex for the right reasons, based on the company's desire to use a flexible structure to create a more engaged benefit offering to answer people's needs, what do you need to consider to determine whether flex is the right structure for you?

- How do you know when to use a flexible benefits structure
- How do you know how to structure it
- To whom do you offer it
- How do you achieve success in communicating it
- When is the right time to move to a flex platform solution?

Though flexible benefit plans have been used since the 1970s, flex in Asia began trending very popular in the employee benefits space only in the last few years. Increasing healthcare costs are becoming a big challenge for many companies. While general inflation rates can and are influenced by government policy, medical inflation rates are not as easily controlled. Rates tend to be on average 5.5% higher than the annual general inflation rate. In some countries the inflation differences exceed 10-14%. ("Global medical trend rate report 2016", Aon Hewitt)

How do companies respond to a driving force this alarming which they cannot impact, affect or keep in check? "The way many employers are approaching this dilemma is by encouraging employees to be stakeholders in their own benefits, whether this is through cost sharing, or introducing flexibility whereby employees can have a greater say in the benefits they have. For employers, greater employee participation can be an important step towards achieving one of their most important strategic benefit objectives: to improve attraction, retention and engagement, and to increase the perceived value that employees have of their benefits." (2015 Asia Pacific Benefit Trends, Towers Watson)

> Flexible benefit programmes allow an employer to predictably forecast and budget for benefit spending by adopting a cost-sharing approach with employees to minimize the impact of yearly cost increases.

Providers and promoters of the structure hail it for its ability to cost-contain but as reported by the Mercer Marsh

Benefits survey of insurance companies in 2015, *Medical Trends around the World*, "only 28% of respondents see employers engaging in implementing flexible benefit programmes to contain heath care costs." Positive impact can be seen when low contribution rates to elect certain benefits may attract employees to options with more cost sharing, and the cost sharing can help contain claims. Adverse or anti-selection effects created in a flexible benefits structure are a challenge for insurers because typically an employee selects benefits that he or she is more likely to need. Employees who are ill more frequently or know they require treatment are more inclined to top-up their medical plan, while employees enjoying good health display relatively low purchase willingness. The result can lead to higher claims per employee selecting each benefit.

There are ways to avoid anti-selection effects but typically this decreases the amount of choice available to employees. A few ways to avoid adverse benefit election is increased pricing or grouping optional benefit selections. Pricing may have an impact on enrolment and therefore leave employees feeling the programme does not offer a cost-effective form of protection, or does not represent good value for money. In addition, grouping coverage selection may leave an employee feeling as though the programme is not flexible enough to meet their needs. For example, they do not need vision care but they do want dental cover and these two benefits only come together. If employees develop this view, the structure may counteract the original intention of flex.

Another way of decreasing the effects of anti-selection as an employer is to enforce lock-in periods during which benefits elected cannot be altered. You may require employees to set their benefits at the start of the year and only offer the opportunity to make changes to their elections at the start of a new year or following specific qualifying lifestyle events, like getting married or having a baby. These events inherently reflect a change in an employee's needs, so allowing people to amend their benefit elections to suit their coverage requirements is appropriate and engaging.

If your workforce is not incredibly large, numbering over 1,000, or the take-up rates or voluntary opt-in figures are low, the risk pooling benefits of your employee numbers may not provide cost savings significant enough to offer a good insurance value proposition for the company or its people. You then lose a major benefit that comes with economy of scale when purchasing protection.

A detailed understanding of the demographic of your member population tends to be one of the main drivers for considering a flexible benefits programme. You should consider the age and gender profile as well as the family status of people within the group, and review the diversity of the members including identifying any significant outliers within the population. When you have a demographically diverse work force, it may appear more difficult to determine whom the majority is and how to structure a benefits programme to respond to their needs. For instance, if you have a large number of employees that cross all generations, from early 20-somethings to mid-60s, all of whom are likely to have different priority lists when it comes to benefit needs and demands, considering a flexible platform may help you offer more choice designed to better meet the needs of all your people. Employers with large employee populations in the thousands with comprehensive compensation and benefit systems, in particular, tend to favour this structure.

In most programmes, employees are able either to retain their existing salary while varying the mix of benefits they receive or adjust their salary up or down by taking fewer or more benefits respectively. There is usually a 'benefit allowance', also called 'flexible spending account, FSA' or 'health spending account, HSA', which is a fixed value provided by the employer on top of salary and benefits which the employee can put towards the cost of their elections. In more complex structures, an employee may be able to buy or sell company-funded benefits using their own salary. Popular options offered are buying or selling annual leave entitlement and reducing or increasing insurance coverage limits. Employers typically determine year to year whether there is any increase to the spending account entitlement and therefore are not in a position where they have to keep pace with alarming rates of medical inflation but can pass some of this increase onto the employee's cost of benefits.

Companies need to understand the tax implications for the salary sacrifice and benefit elections they are providing to employees, both from a corporate perspective and also from a personal perspective, so they can offer a basic understanding of the financial impact to their employees. This is essential in the communication process, especially as the more flexibility that is offered tends to drive higher tax impact on the employee. Depending on state or country tax law, this may differ across your employee population so understanding the compliance and local tax environments is essential.

In line with the new employee and employer landscape of today, people are continuously evaluating the give and take when it comes to benefits. At Expat Insurance, I have seen an increased desire for employees to maximize the benefit spending they receive through FSA or HSA by purchasing private insurances. Given the increased mobility of people in today's global workforce, benefits offered through their employer are seen as inherently linked to their employment. For instance, if you are offered an option to top-up your life insurance coverage and commit some of your allowance to do this only to leave employment two years later, the allowance you had put toward the increased benefit election would be invaluable as that coverage does not follow you and is forfeited.

There is a new trend emerging in which employees have a desire for transferability upon leaving employment. This coverage continuation benefit would offer the employee either a period of time in which they maintain their benefits under the same structure or a modified but similar version of what they were offered while employed. You may also consider offering a choice to change from group benefits to individual benefits for an indefinite period of time following employment. This would encourage employee investment in topping-up their flexible benefit elections under an employer-sponsored programme.

This continuation concept is not new. In 1985, under the Reagan administration in the US, the Consolidated Omnibus Budget Reconciliation Act (COBRA) was passed. COBRA mandates an insurance programme that provides some employees the ability to continue health insurance coverage after leaving employment. As this coverage is inherent and legally mandated in the US, the American market and employees working in the states are familiar with this benefit and therefore expect this to be an option, even if they are employed overseas. Until a few years ago, it was almost unheard of to have this continuation benefit as an offering outside of the US. It is now much more common to engage in discussions with companies about the benefit of coverage continuation if it is aligned with the HR and Benefits Philosophy of the firm.

Without the help of technology, a flexible benefits programme can be a burden on administration. The more flexible the programme and the more elections offered, the more complex the administration. When payroll is impacted based on benefit elections, it is critical to have a seamless internal process or system to avoid payroll blunders costing time, money and morale impact. Flexible benefit programmes require a heavy focus on technology and while the benefits of this programme structure can far outweigh the burden, you need to carefully consider your company's investment objectives and ability to meet the financial requirements for the technology tools to make flex work.

Towers Watson found that "employers across Asia use a variety of methods to communicate with their workforce about benefits — approximately half (49%) use email; 28% use either an online benefit portal or an online total reward statement; and 23% use a paper-based method" (2015 Asia Pacific Benefit Trends, Towers Watson). Considering that only 28% of employers are currently using an online benefit portal to communicate existing programme benefits with people, my guess is investment in technology to administer a programme is even further behind this figure. 23% still push paper.

Flex as a benefit structure can potentially be an ideal answer to address a broad range of needs for people within your organization. It can also engage employees at a more personal level to provide a high impact and well-received programme in line with your HR and Benefits Philosophy and employee value proposition. Communication is critical. Flexible benefits create additional complexity which a more traditional structure avoids. In order for an employee to feel the choice provided to them in a benefits programme is valuable, they need to understand how each of the options may provide and offer them a better or more suitable level of protection or peace of mind. "Despite the success of flexible benefits programmemes in achieving employers' objectives, even the successful schemes face challenges: - Communicating with employees is seen as the biggest challenge, cited by 68%." (Employee Benefits and Trends Survey 2015, Aon)

In my experience at Expat Insurance, our private clients whom engage us for professional advice on understanding their company-sponsored benefits have often been offered no assistance with making their benefit elections. "How would I understand whether or not I need additional coverage and which options I should choose?" is the common question we help people to answer. People only truly understand how to determine what benefit elections are a fit for their needs after hearing an explanation of the baseline of coverage provided, followed by how each top-up option changes the way benefits respond in different scenarios.

Employers must be careful to explain but not advise about benefit choices because companies do not want to take on liability for any adverse effects of benefit selection on the employee.

This fine line creates challenges for businesses, HR leaders and managers alike. How far is too far?

The requirement and investment in tech support, as well as the communication challenges that come with a flexible benefits programme are still proving to be major obstacles in the way employers view a return on their financial investment when it comes to employee benefit programmes. In addition, implementation and administration challenges mean it is very easy for flex to create a disjointed approach which becomes the source of complexity and confusion for many people on your team. "Flexible benefits, once seen as a magic bullet to contain costs while attracting and retaining talent, are reportedly being considered less than many other techniques." (Medical Trends Around the World 2015, Mercer Marsh Benefits)

# Chapter 13

# FLEXIBLE BENEFITS REDEFINED

Voluntary benefits, also known as affinity benefits, are products and services that are available through an employer for purchase by employees, usually at a discounted rate or with preferential benefits linked to their employment. These differ from flexible benefits in that the employee funds one hundred percent of the cost.

For me, the idea of redefining flexible benefits was born out of Expat Insurance's relationship and partnership with Microsoft in Singapore. The offices here have a demographically diverse employee population made up of about 800 people. Microsoft also has a strong HR leadership team who all echo the company's HR and Benefits Philosophy of wantint to provide for their people. Their HR team is committed to engaging employees and explaining the benefits provided under the programme during onboarding, and at times even prior to the employee joining the company.

Microsoft also advertises and hosts optional participation health and wellness days three to four times a year. There is always a presentation of the basic benefits provided to every member of the Microsoft team on the day.

After consistently receiving feedback from employees who attended the health and wellness days, Microsoft knew they had to take action and go above and beyond their existing engagement strategy to support employees who also wanted a resource and advice on arranging private coverage to top-up their existing employee benefits. They took an obvious next step, which was to engage their incumbent broker to assist. This led to frustration. The broker had been secured by shared services and procurement at a global level, and locally the broker was unable to support private client product solutions.

During the health and wellness days, the broker would present the basic employer-sponsored benefits and only illustrate the coverage arranged through the company. Originally, the days were focused on providing a forum to educate and create a culture of trust so that the employees understood the coverage and limitations of their employee benefits. In an effort to increase the transparency of the limitations, we worked with Microsoft to highlight the areas of coverage which may provide gaps and traps for employees. They had enough stories to share of how they exercised "HR guardrails" and wanted a long-term, engaged solution, which we were able to support.

We began attending the health and wellness days and were on call during onboarding when Microsoft HR or their new employees had questions about extending the benefits programme on a private basis. When they could not get answers from their existing broker, they called our team.

Whenever they called, we would work with the employees directly to help explain the benefits. We would also take the time to explain the context of medical expenses for foreigners just relocated or relocating to Singapore. We might explain to an employee that the benefits programme provides them with reimbursement for pregnancy but that the total cost for welcoming a newborn to the world in private care here was going to rack up bills of about $15,000-$20,000. If they were focused on family planning, our team would help them understand their options.

As a result of this approach, we engaged employees with an education-first approach to create a foundation of transparency and trust. We supported Microsoft in their efforts to go above and beyond in providing a resource and offered a personal professional advisory service to their people. At no additional cost, together we helped them redefine the idea of flexible benefits, totally in tune with their population's personal needs. Flex can be about connecting employees with service providers that can help them use their health spending account to provide them with tailored personal solutions at no additional cost to the company.

Creative thinking and innovative services and solutions which flex further than traditional programmes can actually help you provide incredible value for your population. You can offer your employees an opportunity to use their flexible spending power for maximum personal impact. Working in partnership, we redefined flexible benefits beyond what any of their competitors were doing to offer their members a total solution from an employee benefits standpoint.

# Chapter 14

# BENCHMARKING, WHAT'S ALL THE BUZZ ABOUT?

Like flex, benchmarking is another industry buzz word. It has already become etched in an insurance language dictionary. This is a tool that is commonly used by companies to understand their competitive landscape. Understanding how other firms of your size and within your industry manage employee benefit programmes and insight into the benefit limits your competitors offer can provide guidance on how you structure your own programme. Benchmarking only takes into account the external landscape of benefits and says nothing about a company's internal culture code. Let's explore the value of benchmarking and cautions against relying on the tool.

The need to remain competitive is critical given the attraction and retention challenges in today's landscape. Companies must sustain their business' talent demands to grow. If you develop a reputation for offering below market benefits, your recruitment funnel will suffer and hiring challenges will prevail. This could potentially be debilitating for a business of any size. It is for this reason that most large global broking houses and insurance companies hail benchmarking as a significant tool of the trade, one they encourage should help you drive your decision-making process. I personally feel the value of benchmarking has dramatically deteriorated because of the climate change over the last five years.

In all scenarios, benchmarking is dependent on the quality and quantity of data available so it's helpful to ask questions on how benchmarking data is being prepared for presentation. There are only a few resources to assist with compiling competitor data for a benchmarking exercise. The first is an intermediary or provider's own client portfolio which helps you understand market standard as well as firms who are outliers and providing above or below market standard when it comes to benefits. The challenge with these metrics is that comparative data tends to be based on only a small client base of only one particular service provider.

Whitepapers and research companies are an additional resource relied upon. Quality and quantity of data is becoming less accessible for all as it is harder to come by with the increase in small and medium size enterprises with smaller workforce numbers. Therefore, benchmarking is a much more reliable tool which helps you to understand what the biggest employers in the market provide. Also take into account that published industry data typically reports on past trends and patterns and may not be reflective of where companies are going with any definitive direction in the future. The data itself should not be relied upon to provide you with timely and detailed insight into the benefit structures and limits of the companies for today, or of tomorrow.

All the same, large global broking houses and service providers continue to report on the value and reliance of benchmarking. To illustrate this, Aon reports, "The responses on benefit drivers show some interesting shifts in the 2015 survey compared to 2014. Meeting market norms has jumped from fourth place to first, showing that competition between employers, and the need to provide a benefits package that stands up well against those of your peers, is a priority." (Employee Benefits and Trends 2015, Aon)

I maintain that in view of the new generation of employee, benchmarking has begun to lose significant ground as a tool for employers. While I believe that it can add value by providing competitive insight, it should only be referred to as a very general guide during the benefits exercise to ensure you are not missing the mark against the competition.

With the rise of smaller firms and fast growth start-ups whose aim is to be a disruptor in their industries, benchmarking benefits loses even more meaning in the market.

"Approximately twice as many employers refer to market benchmarking to a great extent compared to taking into account employee opinion. This is likely to be the wrong priority for employers looking to maximize value from their benefit programmes." (2015 Asia Pacific Benefit Trends, Towers Watson) In addition, attracting top talent becomes the key focus as these smaller and medium-sized companies take their businesses and brands global. They do not rely on a large workforce of 5,000+ to accomplish their business growth and profitability targets, but on a much smaller talent pool that are high-performing and specialised in their field. Remuneration structures which only seek to meet the benchmark will typically not lure top talent.

Towers Watson echo my sentiment, "As employers evaluate which changes to implement, more than half (56%) report they will review the actions of competitors or industry peers as they develop their organization's health care agenda in 2016. Rather than follow the competition, however, organizations would be more successful at improving performance by adopting solutions that fit their corporate culture, aligning them with their total rewards strategy and supporting the employee value proposition." (2015 Emerging Trends in Health Care, Towers Watson)

As an industry tool, benchmarking has its merits. In the shifting employment landscape, however, it seems as though benchmarking may become obsolete. It should certainly not be used as a tool to drive your decision-making. The best way to achieve competitive advantage is by looking from the inside out.

# Chapter 15

# SWIMMING IN THE PORTFOLIO POOL

For companies with employee populations between three and one hundred members, you need to consider whether a portfolio or experience-rated programmeme is most appropriate. For large companies with over fifty employees, it is typical to operate an experience-rated programmeme. An experience-rated programmeme is one wherein the policy premium is based on consumption and utilization of the benefits each year, calculated on the basis of a loss ratio which is cumulative over the account's years on coverage. In layman terms, claims affect premium.

For small and medium sized firms, it may be more appropriate to consider portfolio or community-rated protection products. This would ensure the policy premium does not change based on the group member claim's experience alone. The insurance company takes into account claim history for all clients within the product portfolio, or for all clients who have purchased the same level of benefits and have a similar number of members in the group. All groups together generate a loss ratio for the portfolio rather than for each client. Premium is then adjusted and all clients will benefit or pay for the utilization rate of the portfolio.

When you swim in the portfolio pool, the idea is that you can access the benefits of a product you may not otherwise have been able to purchase. Typically, it can provide much bigger benefits. This is not specific to the industry. It is not specific to employee headcount. It's specific to products. The concept behind portfolio product is that it is not experience-rated. This means that if you are an employer who has fifteen employees and one of those fifteen receives a cancer diagnosis and subsequent treatment with big bills, your premiums are going to skyrocket in the next year if you are rated based on your own group's experience. Because you are a small group, one claim will exacerbate your loss ratio. If the premium you paid for your policy for fifteen people is $100,000, and you have a $350,000 cancer claim this year alone, clearly the insurance company needs to recoup their costs. The insurer cannot continue to charge $100,000 for the next five years to recover those costs because if another diagnosis comes or the bills for ongoing treatment of the member continue. Please keep in mind this means that the insurance company has to charge more in order to accommodate the known claims which are sure to come. Insurance is about protection of the unknown, but when claims are imminent, the price will certainly reflect this. The insurance company will need to adjust pretty dramatically the next year for a group of only fifteen people, and unfortunately most of the time companies are left in a situation where they have no choice but to accept the premium increase.

There are big benefits to swimming in the portfolio pool. But you should understand and accept the benefits and limitations as a company based on whether this is a good solution for your group or not. Do you want to be up against the risk of having your premium swing dramatically one way or another on the basis of your own employee claims experience? Do you want the protection of purchasing a product that allows you the safety of a much bigger risk pool? It does not mean you need to have an off-the-shelf benefits programme. What is most important is to find an insurance company that recognizes the value for both of you, and sees the relationship and the associated benefits being offered as a partnership. Because you need to understand that if one particular product or benefit table receives a substantial amount of claims, the insurance company will then adjust the premium for that entire portfolio. Not just you, but all of the other companies whom purchased a similar level of benefits as well. We are all in it together, for good and bad, swimming in the portfolio pool is a partnership.

This allows you to lock into a benefit table where if the portfolio performs well in a year, the premiums remain largely stable. Doing this you can avoid facing massive premium swings from one year to the next. Insurance companies can make small adjustments to impact benefits or access only marginally as they see one particular line of benefits being utilized year on year. If the portfolio continues with a standard loss ratio that was projected from that particular line of benefits or type of benefits, then you will have the opportunity to participate in small scalable increases that are in line with inflation and increasing medical costs, and you will have a much more resilient and sustainable programme.

"Employers' affordability concerns are growing as health care costs are increasing at more than twice the rate of inflation — an issue that has persisted for a half century... After relentless increases beyond inflation every year over the last 50 years, health care has become a growing piece of the total rewards pie. And at some companies and in some industries, health care cost increases have been much higher than average for many years." (2015 Emerging Trends in Health Care, Towers Watson) Swimming in the portfolio pool offers a major benefit for smaller companies. Whereas, for much larger companies, with 150+ employees, the group is large enough of a portfolio in itself that the population can afford to swim in their own pool and focus on adjusting benefits and implementing cost containment features where required to mitigate premium increases.

There are benefits afforded to companies and programmes under both an experience-rated and a portfolio-rated model. Much depends on your company's ability to be able to control the benefits within the programme.

There are fewer product options offered under the portfolio-rated model as typically the portfolio approach is based on companies buying a similar level of benefits via off-the-shelf or only slightly modified benefit tables. Some insurers do not even offer a portfolio product solution for groups. Risk pooling allows insurers to provide benefits to companies who opt to take part in a portfolio or community pooling model. Companies wanting more control and a more tailored benefit table will need to be comfortable with an experience-rated programme which means the premium is adjusted each year on the basis of your group's own claims experience.

Understanding the differences as well as the risks and rewards of each model before determining which option is best suited is important when focusing on creating a sustainable solution for your company long-term.

# Chapter 16

# PROFILING HAS POTENTIAL

Let's talk about profiling as an innovative tool fit for the purposes of bringing the industry and your programme into the new age. Of course, profiling can be used as a tool to create both positive and negative impact. When is it valuable to you and your efforts during the benefits exercise? When can it be detrimental?

The positive is that when we profile employee populations on the basis of different metrics - size, demographic or occupation - there may be benefit to segmenting certain employee populations in the course of your benefits exercise. Consolidating people and groups with similar characteristics or risk profiles may provide substantial benefit when pooling. Likewise, an employee population who has a large cross-section of risk profiles can be big benefit as we can pool high risk with lower risk: for instance airline crew with senior management whom are in administrative roles. This strategy is wrought with challenges, especially when it comes to an insurer's understanding of how to underwrite and price a programme, but the use of innovative tools does not always come free and easy.

## Unique Occupational Factors

Let's begin by focusing on a population with unique occupational factors, like those in the oil and gas industry. There tend to be similar benefit requirements due to the inherent job nature and profile of an offshore employee population. On a rig, vessel, platform or FPSO, rotations are the norm so coverage typically responds only when on or off rotation. We also frequently find additional support services like a doctor or nurse practitioner onboard and available to support the offshore population. Routine health screenings which are industry requirements also ensure the group is generally healthy without the challenge of chronic and recurring illness.

When you drill down and identify that there are employee populations within an industry who have very similar profiles, you can actually create a portfolio or a risk pool based on this profile. When you build a big enough portfolio of these kinds of groups, you create value through the use of a scheme, affinity or specialized suite of products suited to the population's unique profile. The major benefit here comes in offering voluntary or opt-in protection in addition to your core benefits structure. To do this, the portfolio usually needs to be much larger than the population of just one company. You need access to a bigger group to risk pool and offer you a reduction in premium based on a tailored benefit offering suited to the unique needs of this segment of a population. The larger group would typically encompass more than one company's workforce. Therefore there is protection against one firm's higher claims and utilization culture by pairing it with another's unclaimed record.

## Employee Population Profiles

I have focused on helping clients and insurance companies recognize when there are population profiles that are remarkably less unique which could benefit from being consolidated to create value in the same way. This is incredibly successful within the small business, SME, community in particular. Consider all the start-ups with employee populations of less than fifty people. By consolidating and assisting a large group of these firms, we can wrap up a lot of small employee populations to create product offerings and appetite within the insurance market where there has been none.

For instance, you might have more than a few unwilling insurance companies that do not offer maternity coverage to firms with an employee headcount of under fifteen people. Given that the desire for companies to purchase this cover usually means the risk of paying substantial claims is almost guaranteed, there may be a lack of appetite in the industry to accommodate coverage. By bringing together many companies of a similar size, we can create a risk pool where there would not otherwise be one and offer comfort to the insurer that when they offer the benefits in demand, the solution can be sustainable. We can wrap the employee populations of multiple companies together to leverage the value of economy of scale, for the benefit of all.

> Profiling in an effort to pool can encourage carriers to offer benefits which may not have otherwise been made available to you.

This need not be done in such a formal or structured way where you as a company commit to joining the pool. Getting creative and building partnerships across the industry, I have generated appetite and interest in areas where some insurers would have felt otherwise entirely uncomfortable. Bold new ways of thinking can bring big benefits to the business of employee benefits.

Profiling can also be a tool that works against you. I remind you of the story I shared in Chapter 7, where my client assumed that because they were getting a specialty package for insurance in the oil and gas industry that coverage would be comprehensively suited to their needs. When an insurance company uses profiling in their interests, they use their understanding of a specific industry or segment of a population to design programme structures. They may create specialized exclusions which apply only to your people. For example, an insurance provider who understands the demands of an offshore workforce which may have a high incident of certain conditions or a bigger need for specific benefits in a programme may underwrite out of coverage in these areas. If you follow the blueprint, you should uncover these insurers, products and exclusions during the benefits exercise so you can avoid any problems caused by profiling in advance of implementing a programme.

When profiling is used as a leveraging tool for clients it can create incredibly positive impact. Contrary to belief, it does not pigeonhole you. Instead, it opens the door wider to the availability of programmes, benefits and insurance partners.

# Section 4

## INSIDE THE INDUSTRY

# Chapter 17

# INSURANCE COMPANIES

Once you have structured your benefits programme in Step 2, the Benefits Exercise, you need to place the insurance coverage with the right carrier. This can be an intense part of the process, especially if you are working under tight timelines. But take your time, as knowing and understanding the market and the insurance companies operating in market is critical to success. It is important to consider the following:

- The technical capabilities of each insurance company
- Their risk appetite
- Administrative procedures
- Online tools and apps
- After-sales support services

A strong programme design placed with an inappropriate choice of insurer will lead to unexpected and unanticipated challenges which can be devastating to overcome during the course of the policy year. It can create and fuel employee frustrations. Even if the programme design is aligned with your HR and Benefits Philosophy, if in the course of accessing their benefits and making claims, members have a bad experience, these interactions can lead to morale management matters and leave people feeling disengaged with the programme.

Be aware that insurance companies may have different benefits, products and service capabilities in different parts of the world. This can be based on licensing, actuarial prowess and compliance constraints in certain markets. When you structure a programme for a globally mobile workforce, the right insurance partner is key. Local knowledge about all of the partners available to you during the programme placement stage should not be overlooked.

The insurance industry is a master of big data and actuarial science, leveraging every data point about the statistics of health, illness, accident, life and death to model probability and profitability. Gauging what benefits each insurer is prepared to offer and at what price allows you to structure and negotiate the best value for money solutions.

There are many ways to tailor a benefits table to suit the needs of the company. Not every insurer makes all options available or shares openly all of the different ways in which you can tweak coverage. As a general guide, you can:

- Add or remove benefits
- Increase or decrease limits or sum insured
- Implement co-insurance or co-pays
- Include or exclude specific conditions or treatment
- Modify policy wording adding endorsements, extensions or exclusions
- Add room or provider restrictions
- Offer sub-limits
- Limit number of visits
- Require referrals or pre-authorisation
- Claim reimbursement options.

If you are working with insurers whom are receptive to tailoring the benefits table, you are able to modify the benefits offered in the programme to suit your needs. Customizing coverage offers more flexibility in the pricing and can really open negotiations positively.

Open communication is paramount in building your programme and partnerships; between the insurance provider and your company liaison, whether it is an HR or business leader, an office manager or your broker. As Karen Clifford observed and commented, in her experience, "[But] what we didn't have is a partnership and this is why I think there is a missing link. Typically, benefits providers do one thing, employers do another thing; They need to get smarter about how they work together." The partnership aspect is crucial and success in this area impacts how you as an employer are able to provide better benefits and protection for your people.

# Chapter 18

## INTERVIEWING INTERMEDIARIES

Insurance and financial services is a technically complex industry. While leaders in your business best understand your people, your culture, your Benefits Philosophy and business strategy, an intermediary can be relied upon to provide the technical resources required when structuring your insurance programmes. Stephanie Nash echoed this in her interview, "A broker is critical, they are an additional resource which help you negotiate, place and administer the programme. This is not typically within the core competency of an HR team and even if it costs more, this role is best outsourced."

The vast world of insurance providers, brokers and intermediaries can be a minefield. Where do you begin in your search for the right partner? As reported in the Employee Benefits and Trends Survey 2015, "When it comes to identifying potential new suppliers, recommendations are by far the most popular source, with 88% using others' experience to find possible providers. 52% would use a web search, with 46% finding potential providers at events. 42% use industry magazines as a source of provider information." (Employee Benefits and Trends Survey 2015, Aon) Within your network you will hear horror stories and hopefully you will hear rave reviews of intermediaries as well. Start by asking around, word of mouth can be a powerful tool in helping you select the right partner to work with.

Given the technical complexity of the industry and the impact advisors may have on consumer confidence and regulatory credibility, in most countries across the globe, the insurance industry is heavily governed by the fiscal authorities of the land. This fact can offer you significant insight and guidance on who everyone is and what their roles are within the industry. After all, you want someone who works for you to help you simplify this process.

As industry jargon can create additional complexity in your hunt for the right partnership, I have included this glossary as a guide to help you define most roles and their associated interests in plain terms.

**Tied Agent** • An individual or company licensed to sell only one insurance company's products. They work for the insurance company directly and are not able to advise you on any other products or services. Usually associated with a direct distribution model or direct to consumer sales team.

**Agent, Agency or Corporate Agency** • An individual or company licensed to work with a small number of firms, usually up to three. They work for the insurance companies directly and are not able to advise you on any other products or services. They are licensed to sell only the products of their associated insurance companies and cannot discuss competitor products or market landscape with you.

**Broker** • An independent firm licensed to work as a whole-of-market service provider. A broker has access to all insurance companies. They employ individuals who may be licensed to sell all products or only specialized products, dependent on their qualifications. They work for you, the client, and can advise on all products and services.

**Bancassurance** • When insurance companies want to use banks as a distribution source, they will partner together and either offer the same product or, more often, a modified product option to the market. Any number of people within the bank may be able to assist you: the tellers, account relationship managers or a specialized insurance team. Usual products sold via the bancassurance model are: mortgage insurance and travel insurance. This same model applies to credit card companies who partner in the same way as the banks do to offer their customer base products as either supplements, special benefits or ancillary and ride-on packages to the credit card services they supply.

**Direct** • An insurance company or third party product provider.

You need to be in the driver's seat when it comes to finding the right fit with a technical partner. Arming yourself with the right questions is key. Note that in every country there may be deviations to these categories. But remember this one simple line which will help you get to the heart of what you want to know: who do you work for? Understanding whether a partner acts in your interests or has other competing interests will provide you with the transparency you need and is a great place to start building trust together.

In today's business battleground it goes without saying that the fewer competing interests a company has governing their motivations the better. Independence allows a service provider the ability to help you understand competitive landscape. An intermediary can help keep insurance companies and product providers in check every step of the way without draining your own internal resources - recall the story in Chapter 6 of the international school whom was paid up with no protection.

When it comes to buying insurance, insurers and product providers typically have to define their high level distribution strategies with the regulator. They can either choose to work direct to consumer with no intermediaries involved, a combination of direct to consumer and intermediaries or they can work solely through distributors with no option for the client to buy direct. In Singapore and in many other countries, if an insurance company elects to use any form of intermediated distribution channel, they cannot discount premium to encourage customers to buy direct. In Singapore, this is enforced to preserve a customer-centric industry and ensure credibility and integrity in the industry. You can shop with confidence in these markets as there are few competing interests with independent intermediaries. And best of all, there is no added cost.

# Chapter 19

# CHRONICLES OF INNOVATION

I want to share some of our success stories to illustrate how easy it is to change the game and implement innovative and creative approaches for your organization.

### Coverage Needs And Standard Market Products Collide Causing Costs to Catapult

BASIC SUMMARY OF OUR CLIENT'S NEEDS: Coverage for both the locally-hired employees as well as for the expatriate management team and their families. The company had regional presence across Asia with operations in Singapore, Malaysia, Thailand and Indonesia. People frequently travelled to America as well as remote locations. Work included high-risk activities, both onshore and offshore.

HEADCOUNT: 18 employees at initial engagement

**CHALLENGE:** Standard market products mean benefit duplication across multiple products. Client is over-insured but the only other option is self-insuring risk which they cannot afford if it came to a claim.

Following initial engagement, we took the client through the benefit blueprint. Specific focus was given to prioritizing their needs and reviewing their existing coverage. We mapped out the premium increases over prior years, conducted a loss ratio review and analyzed benefit utilization rates.

**HOW WE CAME TO THE RESCUE:** A flexible benefits programme was developed which helped avoid over-insurance and achieve cost-effective protection for all their needs. The programme which was implemented, including self-insured benefits, is managed and administered by our team who engage as an extension of our client's operation.

- A two-tiered medical insurance benefits programme

- Local Tier: an industry-competitive locally-focused product which provided inpatient benefits and outpatient benefits with an annual limit and co-payment, offering regional location consolidation for employees only

- Management Tier: comprehensive inpatient and outpatient benefits which covered travel worldwide with the exclusion of USA and no deductible or co-payment. We could offer consolidation for all their offices in the region, including employees and dependents

- Self-insured dental reimbursement scheme
- Self-insured wellness incentive programme which offered reimbursement for co-payment to employees on the Local Tier
- Corporate travel policy for employees: tailored benefits which excluded medical expenses and included search and rescue response
- Top-up travel insurance was made available for purchase online on a per-trip or annual basis for dependents (cost not sponsored or subsidized by employer)
- A select team of Private Client advisors were appointed to assist dependents of the locally-hired employees with arranging health insurance policies. The policies were issued privately to these individuals (cost not sponsored or subsidized by employer)

**Growth Exceeds Expectations, Employee Benefits Budget Required Recalibration**

BASIC SUMMARY OF OUR CLIENT'S NEEDS AND THE CHALLENGE: Employee population experiences a 60% increase in headcount mid-term and the HR team is tasked with revising the employee benefit programme on a decreased budget to deflate expenses, and keeping business growth targets on track.

**HEADCOUNT** • 45 employees at initial engagement. Even more pleased to report our client's business success continued and they now number over 250

**GO GUERILLA:** We went guerilla with renewal negotiations. While a decrease in benefits was unavoidable, we focused on maintaining the look and feel of the programme from the employee perspective in order to minimize the negative impact of a change in benefits internally.  As we entered renewal negotiations, we arranged a meeting with the insurance company's underwriting team and discussed the viability of our proposed recommendations to tailor the programme to achieve the reduction in premium we were working towards.  Armed with statistics on the account's profitability over the prior 3 years in hand, our office was able to achieve a premium decrease of 20%. By migrating appropriate service responsibilities from the carrier to our firm - initial claim assessment, doctor and hospital liaison for pre-arranged inpatient treatment and support for member's email inquiries - we were able to negotiate a further premium reduction of 10%.  A modified benefit programme was presented to employees by our firm at the same time the company announced their annual growth figures. With total transparency on the reasons behind the changes, positive feedback was received. After all, achieving stronger than expected business results is as good for employees as it is for business. Sharing became part of a successful employee benefits strategy.

**Corporate Benefits Crunch Leaves Employees Running For Cover**

BASIC SUMMARY OF OUR CLIENT'S NEEDS: Assist with an outcry of inquiries on top-up health insurance benefits and quell confusion.

HEADCOUNT: 2,500 members at initial engagement

SHELTER FROM THE STORM: Following the financial crisis, companies looked to cost-cut and employee benefit programmes became one of the casualties. With a large portion of MNC employees being expatriate assignees, an organization with a predominant membership of MNCs approached Expat Insurance to develop a solution which would provide capabilities to service membership inquiries and provide health insurance advisory services direct to members.

We opened an umbrella of protection by creating a partnership. We focused first on how our organizations could best fit together and add value based on the new membership needs. We then designed and launched a total solution:

- A co-branded website to alleviate the burden of fielding inquiries, which directed members straight to our team seamlessly

- Education initiatives, including seminars, lunch-and-learns and panel speaking engagements by industry experts

- A membership-exclusive Health Insurance Affinity Programme, offering discounted rates on individual and company plans as well as preferential underwriting terms and conditions. The programme allows transferability into the scheme for current members without alteration to their coverage and offered a product with modular flexibility to create a protection solution for each individual, be it a family or a business, based on their specific needs.

# Conclusion

## BULLETPROOF IN A
## BRAVE NEW WORLD

There has never been a better time in history for companies to start their business or take their brand global. You rely on highly talented people to travel the world to build your brand. Keeping employee benefit programmes aligned with your organization, your people, your leadership, your goals and your competition requires you to stay committed to the Benefits Blueprint. From setting your HR and Benefits Philosophy, to structuring the programme, creating an infrastructure to empowering employees and conducting an annual review you can ensure a sustainable and successful programme.

Creating a strong culture of trust in your company, whether you have eight or eight thousand employees, will be your best armor. Following the five steps in the Benefits Blueprint will ensure you do not lose sight of the path to a successful programme. Of course, while you follow the Blueprint, be sure to seek out help and find the right partners to alleviate complexity and provide guidance along the way.

In this ever-changing employment landscape, communication and partnership is key to success, for everyone. It can transform how you attract, engage and retain talent. The best results come when programmes are insight-driven and data-powered. It is my hope that the content in these chapters helps lift the mystery and show you what is inside the industry when it comes to your options and how to build better benefits. The Benefits Blueprint should empower you to take action and have the confidence and know-how to produce sustainable programmes that answer the needs of your people. For me, just to know that I have helped – and continue to help – innumerable clients navigate their way to securing the right protection energizes me every day.

The more clear you are on your HR and Benefits Philosophy, the stronger your foundation will be as you follow the steps of the blueprint. Your Benefits Exercise will be comprehensive, leaving no stone unturned. An infrastructure will be set up that is supportive yet flexible in the face of unforeseen shifts in your industry, workforce, or the world. Flawless communication and total employee engagement will be achievable. Finally, you will have your review and renewal processes in place, guaranteeing transparency, accountability, and a commitment to consistency.

Employee benefits help you look after your most valuable assets, your people. With great people comes great responsibility. Dare to be different and use the tools delivered in this book to challenge the status quo. Building better benefits will make you bulletproof in this brave new world.

# NOTES

# NOTES

Made in the USA
Las Vegas, NV
19 February 2025

18395838R00098